Grammar Made Simple

Grade 5

Written by Sara Freeman
Illustrated by Roberta Collier-Morales
Cover Illustration by Anita Dufalla

Notice! Copies of student pages may be reproduced by the classroom teacher for classroom use only, not for commercial resale. No part of this publication may be reproduced for storage in a retrieval system, or transmitted in any form or by any means—electronic, mechanical, recording, etc.—without the prior written permission of the publisher. Reproduction of these materials for an entire school or school system is strictly prohibited.

FS123304 Grammar Made Simple Grade 5
All rights reserved–Printed in the U.S.A.
Copyright © 2000 Frank Schaffer Publications
23740 Hawthorne Blvd.
Torrance, CA 90505

Table of Contents

Introduction 1

Sentences   2–19

    Teacher Ideas 2–9

    Student Reproducibles 10–19

Parts of Speech   20–41

    Teacher Ideas 20–29

    Student Reproducibles 30–41

Usage   42–57

    Teacher Ideas 42–47

    Student Reproducibles 48–57

Mechanics   58–74

    Teacher Ideas 58–62

    Student Reproducibles 63–74

Answer Key 75–78

Introduction

Teaching children to speak and write effectively is a key component of a well-rounded education. Grammar is the cornerstone of that teaching. Children's questions show they want to know the how and why of oral and written communication.

Do I write a business letter the same way I do a friendly letter?

What does "ml" mean?

Doesn't "its" need an apostrophe?

Why can't I say "We played good"?

Frank Schaffer's *Grammar Made Simple Grade 5* is designed to give students a strong foundation in language skills. The book contains teacher ideas for whole-class activities, group activities, and partner activities. In addition, there are reproducible student pages designed for practicing specific skills or for use as a reference.

There are four sections in this book: Sentences, Parts of Speech, Usage, and Mechanics (Capitalization and Punctuation). Because the topics are interrelated, you may choose to introduce them out of order. Let your students' strengths and weaknesses guide you in selecting which topics to focus on.

Many adults can sense if their writing is correct because it "sounds right." Therefore, a multitude of oral language activities is included to help students speak correctly and develop an ear for correct grammar. This will also develop your students' confidence in speaking and make the concepts come alive for them.

Grammar instruction does not have to be dull and dry. *Grammar Made Simple Grade 5* helps you engage different styles of learners in fun and meaningful activities.

Sentences

The sentence is the basic unit in writing. Learning the structure of sentences, as well as the different types, will help students communicate in speaking and in writing. Once your fifth graders have mastered the basics, they can learn to reorder, combine, and expand their sentences to make them more complex and interesting.

SENTENCE HUNT
Partner Activity

Direct pairs of students to bring in five different examples of printed materials that are ready to be recycled—pamphlets, magazine ads, business cards, catalog pages, cereal box panels, yellow pages from a phone book, and so on. Have each pair glue its printed materials to a large piece of butcher paper. Review with students what makes a sentence. (Sample definition: *A sentence tells a complete thought. It has a subject and an action. It begins with a capital letter and ends with a period, question mark, or exclamation mark.*) Next have students read and analyze the different writing samples and label them *sentence* or *not a sentence*. Hold a discussion with students about when and why complete sentences are used and when and why they are not. Encourage them to imagine if every form of writing were in complete sentences, and then if no forms of writing were in complete sentences.

SENTENCE OR NOT?
Partner Activity

"Niagara" by Carl Sandburg

"Niagara Falls" from <u>World Book Encyclopedia</u>

Write poems on the chalkboard or overhead projector to read aloud with your students. "The Mysterious Cat" by Vachel Lindsey in *Sing a Song of Popcorn* (Scholastic, 1988) is a fun one to share. Compare and contrast poems with sentences. Point out that sentences have subjects and actions and tell complete thoughts. Ask students what characteristics poems feature and how they differ from sentences. (Poems often use rhythm, rhyme, or repetition to convey a mood or message. Punctuation and capitalization in poetry differs from that in prose.) Challenge pairs of students to find and copy poems they like about animals or objects. Then have them find and copy factual paragraphs from reference books about the same topics. Have students label and glue the two pieces side by side on construction paper. Display the papers on a bulletin board.

FS123304 Grammar Made Simple Grade 5 • © Frank Schaffer Publications, Inc.

WHAT A SENTENCE!
Group Activity

Have students work in groups of four for this activity. Each person in the group writes one word on a piece of scratch paper. Then everyone reads the different words and writes complete sentences that include all four words. You can adapt the activity to correspond to types of sentences. For example, each student must use all the words in an interrogative sentence.

ASK ME A QUESTION
Group Activity

Give students practice asking questions (interrogative sentences). Divide the class into small groups. Have one student in the group choose a famous person or character to pretend to be. Direct the other students in the group to ask that student questions. The "famous person" must answer the questions in complete sentences. Switch roles every few minutes until all students have had a chance to be famous.

HEY, I WANT TO READ THIS!
Class Activity

Writing introductory paragraphs is a valuable skill that needs to be developed through periodic practice. Model introductory paragraphs that hook the reader by reading passages from articles in children's magazines, such as *Ranger Rick*, *National Geographic World*, or *Sports Illustrated for Kids*. Discuss with students what each paragraph features that makes the reader want to continue. (Many lead paragraphs will include questions or exclamations as well as declarative sentences. Point out the sentence variety as you see it.)

Next, give students this boring example of an introductory paragraph for a report. Fill in the blanks substituting different topics—the Boston Tea Party, soccer, a koala, and so on.

<u>(Topic)</u> *is very interesting. This report will tell all about* <u>(topic)</u>.

Challenge students to create an introductory paragraph for a report topic that makes the reader want to read the report. You can do this activity in conjunction with an assigned report or as a lesson in preparation for reports to be done later.

DO THIS! DO THAT!
Group Activity

Teach or review with students that imperative sentences are commands. Inform students that imperative sentences often omit the subject and begin with a verb. State this example and ask students who they think the subject is: *Go to your room.* (The subject is understood to be *You.*) Give students practice writing commands. First have them make lists of five commands they do not like to hear. Then have them write five more they would like to be able to give. Let students meet in groups to read and compare commands.

CAN YOU DRAW THIS?

Class Activity

Here's a fun activity for writing directions (imperative sentences). Each student will need 10 pennies. Tell students to secretly arrange their pennies in shapes or designs where each penny is touching at least one other penny. Next have students write directions for making the arrangements and draw sketches of them on separate sheets of paper. Then let them exchange papers with partners and follow the directions for assembling the penny shapes. End by having students discuss, revise, and proofread their directions as needed to create finished direction sheets. You can leave the sheets and pennies at an activity table for students to work on during free time.

HOW DID YOU SAY THAT?

Partner Activity

Write this sentence on the chalkboard: *My face is green.* Invite a volunteer to read it aloud. Next change the period to a question mark: *My face is green?* Have another volunteer read it aloud. Then change the question mark to an exclamation mark and have a third student read the sentence aloud: *My face is green!* Talk about how one's intonation changes when speaking statements, questions, or exclamations. Then have students work with partners. One partner writes a sentence without end punctuation and reads it aloud with expression. The other partner determines if the sentence was said as a statement, a question, or an exclamation. Let pairs repeat and continue the activity, switching roles each time.

Homework

1. Which age groups use the most commands?
2. Which age groups ask the most questions?
3. When do people use exclamations?
4. Do you think kids and adults change the way they speak depending on the age of the person with whom they are talking?

Be a Conversation Detective!

Try this homework activity after your class has studied a variety of sentences—statements, questions, commands, and exclamations. Direct students to listen over a week long period to the speech patterns of different-aged people, such as toddlers, children, teenagers, young adults, and older adults. If students do not have a younger sibling or teenager in their families, they may want to listen to words spoken in public places, such as on a playground, at a grocery store, or on a bus.

Challenge students to analyze which types of sentences different ages of people use most. You may want to give them the questions shown here or similar ones and have them take notes. Hold a class discussion afterwards to discuss the results.

IN THE NEWS
Partner Activity

Introduce the topic of subjects and predicates using newspaper headlines. Explain that the subject part of the headline tells whom or what the news story is about and the predicate part tells what the subject is, does, did, or will do. Hold up the front page of your local newspaper. Read aloud the headlines. Each time ask, *Whom or what is this story about?* Use a crayon to circle those words—the subject. Then ask, *What is the subject doing?* Use a crayon to underline those words—the predicate. If possible, point out a headline that is missing a subject or predicate, such as *Rebuilding After Killer Tornado*. Help students recognize which part is missing. (The subject—the name of the community that is rebuilding.) Then give pairs of students sections of the newspaper. (You may use multiple copies of the current day's paper or back issues collected over a few weeks.) Have partners read the headlines and identify the parts, circling the subjects and underlining the predicates.

SUBJECTS 1-10
Partner Activity

1. Cars
2. Our minivan
3. The first automobile
4. An old station wagon
5. A classic Ford Mustang convertible
6. My grandmother's four-wheel drive Explorer
7. A fancy, black limousine with tinted windows
8. A midnight blue Jaguar with gray leather interior
9. A police car with lights flashing and sirens blaring
10. The ugliest, junkiest clunker to ever roll down the road

Give students practice writing subjects with this activity. Direct pairs of students to choose topics and write 10 subjects about them, ranging in length from 1–10 words. Later have pairs exchange papers with another group and write a predicate of any length to finish each sentence.

MAKE IT FUN
Group Activity

If your students complain that studying subjects and predicates is boring, challenge them to make up sentences to work with that are more interesting. Divide the class into small groups. Have each group member in turn name a mood, such as silly, scary, sad, or disgusting. The remaining group members should write creative subjects or predicates to match the mood. Let each group mix and match its subjects and predicates to make some "really good" sentences to submit to you. Use the student-created sentences in lessons or mini-quizzes that relate to subjects and predicates.

RELAY PRACTICE
Class Activity

Teach or review that the complete subject is all the words that tell whom or what the sentence is about while the simple subject is usually the one main word in the subject. Then give your class listening practice with this game. Divide the class into five teams. Have each team send one person to the chalkboard. Read aloud twice a sentence from a story. Direct each student at the chalkboard to write the complete subject and circle the simple subject. Give teams 2 points if both parts of the answer are correct, 1 point if only one part is correct, and 0 points if both parts are wrong. Have teams send new players to the board each round. You can adapt the activity to practice complete and simple predicates as well.

PHOTO FUN

Group Activity

Have students work in groups of three, and give each group a magazine. One student chooses a photograph or illustration and names the subject for a set of sentences about it. (Example: *These seven little ducklings*) The second student writes two sentences about the picture that begin with the same subject but have different predicates with different verbs. Example: *These seven little ducklings fluff up their feathers. These seven little ducklings wait for their mother to return.* Next the third student must combine the two sentences into one longer sentence. Tell students to create a compound predicate using *and* or *or* to connect the verbs. Example: *These seven little ducklings fluff up their feathers and wait for their mother to return.* Let groups complete the activity three times so each person can do each role.

STATE RIDDLES

Partner Activity

Mix U.S. geography with compound sentences in this activity. First model the activity for students using the steps below and the examples given here. Elicit ideas from students as you complete step 3. Then have students work with partners to create their own state riddles. Display the finished riddles around a U.S. map, inviting students to read and solve them during free time.

1. Study a U.S. map and secretly choose a state.
2. Write 10 short clues about your state that begin with the words *I* or *My*.
3. Think of ways to combine the short clues into longer compound sentences, using connecting words like *and, or,* and *but.* You may want to rephrase the clues while doing that.
4. Write a total of six clues that include both simple and compound sentences. End with the question, *Which state am I?*
5. Proofread your sentences. Check that there is a comma before conjunctions that connect what could be two short sentences.
6. For an answer sheet, draw the outline of your state and label it on a separate sheet of paper. Staple your riddle over this.
7. Post your riddle on a bulletin board to share it with your classmates.

Draft (South Dakota)
My name ends with the letter a.
I am larger than Pennsylvania.
I am smaller than Montana.
I have two words in my name.
I border six other states.
I do not have the word New in my name.
I have the Missouri River running through me.
I do not border the state of Missouri.
I am northeast of Arizona.
I am northwest of Alabama.

Final Copy
My name ends with the letter a.
I am larger than Pennsylvania and smaller than Montana.
I am northeast of Arizona and northwest of Alabama.
I do not have the word New in my name, but my name does have two words.
I have the Missouri River running through me, but I do not border the state of Missouri.
I border six other states.
Which state am I?

South Dakota

GRAMMAR ROBOT TO THE RESCUE — Class Activity

Write a few run-on sentences on the chalkboard. Then pretend you are "Grammar Robot" and move in a jerky fashion next to the sentences. Using a robotlike voice, model for students how to correct the run-ons, either dividing them into two short sentences or keeping them as one long sentence with a comma and conjunction connecting the two clauses. Next let a student volunteer write a new run-on sentence at the board. Invite another student to be Grammar Robot and come to the board to correct the run-on sentence. Repeat this activity periodically throughout the year for a fun review.

> **Run-on:** My cat is old he is slow now.
> **Correct:** My cat is old. He is slow now.
> or
> My cat is old, and he is slow now.
>
> **Run-on:** Mark likes swimming and I like swimming and Casey likes skating.
> **Correct:** Mark and I like swimming. Casey likes skating.
> or
> Mark and I like swimming, but Casey likes skating.

HOW SHORT? HOW LONG? — Class Activity

Help students realize that strong writers use sentences of varying lengths. A story or article with all short sentences would be choppy and annoying. Likewise, a piece with every sentence long and winding will bog down a reader. Have students choose single pages from chapter books they are reading. Direct them to count and record the number of words in each sentence on the pages. Then have them copy the shortest and longest sentences. Have students meet in small groups to discuss their findings. Let students apply the lesson to their own work by counting the length of their sentences during the draft phase of writing projects.

> *The Watsons Go to Birmingham—1963*
> by Christopher Paul Curtis   Page 58
>
> *Number of words in each sentence:* 19, 13, 6, 42, 18, 26, 39, 5, 13, 3, 7, 2, 10, 10, 12, 5, 17
>
> *Shortest sentence:* "Come on."
>
> *Longest sentence:* "Sooner or later Momma was going to notice I only had one glove, and ever since I'd found out that half of my blood was that thin Southern kind I'd started wondering if frostbite really could do some damage to my hands."

MAKE THEM FLOW — Class Activity

Using transition words in sentences and paragraphs is another practice good writers employ. Transition words help the reader understand and move forward through the piece of writing. Write a few transition words on a large sheet of butcher paper, decorated to look like a pencil. Then let students brainstorm additional ones. Post the pencil in an area where students can refer to it when drafting and revising their sentences.

Transition Words	*Time Words*—before, during, after, when, first, second, next, then, lastly, finally, soon, later, meanwhile *Compare or Contrast Words*—like, likewise, similarly, in the same way, as well as, but, however, nevertheless, yet, still, although *Concluding Words*—therefore, finally, lastly, in summary

DIAGRAMING SENTENCES

Diagraming sentences is a way of helping students analyze sentence parts. In order to diagram sentences, your students will need to be familiar with the different parts of speech. The following examples will help you review or learn how to diagram. They progress in difficulty. For a class activity, write an example on the chalkboard and explain how it is diagramed. Have students copy the example and then write and diagram three similar sentences of their own.

Simple Sentence   *Dogs drool.*

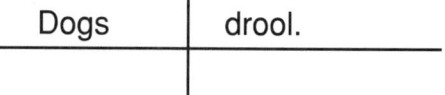

A horizontal line is drawn and then a vertical line. The noun that makes up the subject is written before the vertical line. The verb that makes up the predicate is written after the vertical line.

Compound Subject   *Greyhounds and whippets race.*

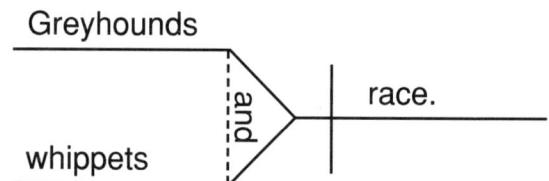

The subject section has two horizontal lines, one above the other. They are connected by a dashed line where the conjunction is written.

Compound Predicate   *Puppies play and dig.*

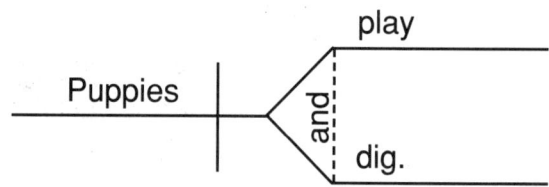

The predicate section has two horizontal lines, one above the other. They are connected by a dashed line where the conjunction is written.

Adjectives   *The frisky husky leaped.*

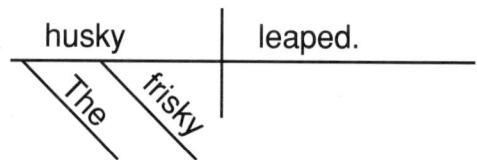

An adjective is written on a diagonal line below the noun it describes.

Adverbs   *The hound bayed loudly.*

   Dogs hear very well.

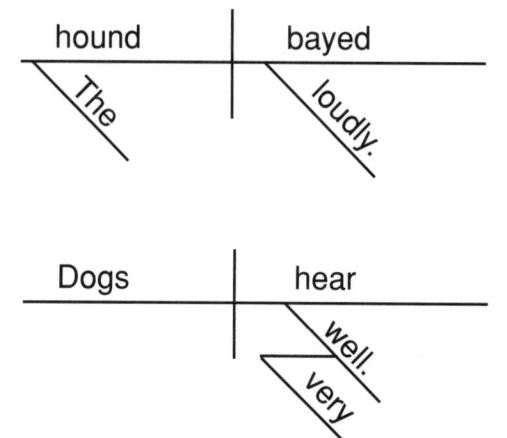

An adverb is written on a diagonal line below the verb it modifies. If an adverb modifies an adjective or another adverb, it is written on a diagonal line and connected by a horizontal line to the word it modifies.

FS123304 Grammar Made Simple Grade 5 • © Frank Schaffer Publications, Inc.

Predicate Adjectives   *The mother dog was quite busy.*

The collie seemed confused and worried.

A predicate adjective follows a linking verb and describes the subject. A predicate adjective is separated from the linking verb by a diagonal line.

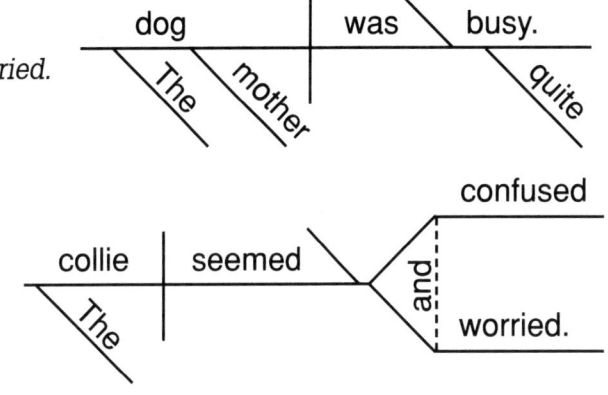

Predicate Nouns   *The chihuahua is the smallest dog.*

A predicate noun follows a linking verb and identifies or explains the subject. A predicate noun is separated from the linking verb by a diagonal line.

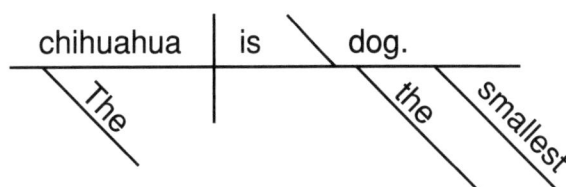

Direct Object   *The puppy chased its tail.*

Police dogs find drugs and explosives.

A direct object is a noun or pronoun that receives the action of the verb. A direct object is separated from the verb by a vertical line that does not cross the horizontal line.

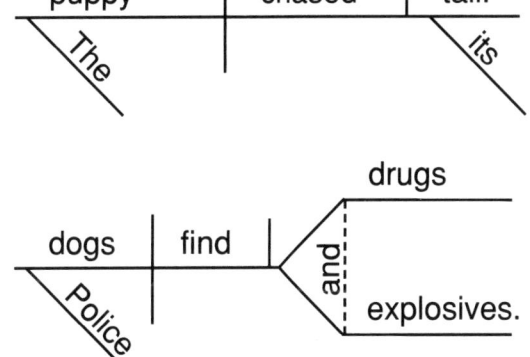

Indirect Object   *My dog brought me a slobbery ball.*

The vet gave the poodle a rabies shot.

An indirect object tells to whom or for whom the action of the verb is done. It comes after the verb and before the direct object. An indirect object is written on a horizontal line below the verb and is connected to it by a diagonal line.

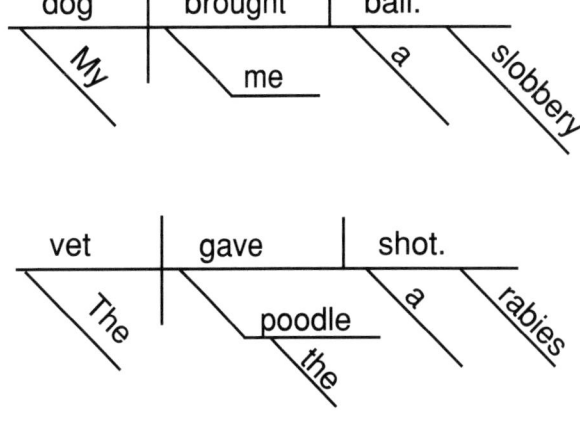

FS123304 Grammar Made Simple Grade 5 ▪ © Frank Schaffer Publications, Inc.

All Through the Year

A **sentence** is a group of words that tells a complete thought.

Read each item. Write **S** if it is a sentence. Write **N** if it is not a complete sentence. Then choose three of the items that you marked **N**. Rewrite them as complete sentences.

<u>S</u> A. The calendar system we use has 12 months.

<u>N</u> B. August is my favorite month because.

___ 1. School is closed on the first day of January.

___ 2. A cold, gray, February day.

___ 3. Where my aunt lives, March is the snowiest month.

___ 4. The worst thing about April Fool's Day.

___ 5. Taught us how to do a Maypole dance.

___ 6. My family goes camping in June.

___ 7. The Fourth of July.

___ 8. My brother's birthday is August 15.

___ 9. The leaves start to change colors in September.

___ 10. Because Halloween is in October.

___ 11. Thanksgiving is the fourth Thursday in November.

___ 12. Last year in December.

<u>B. August is my favorite month because I like hot weather.</u>

_____

_____

_____

_____

_____

What Will Happen?

Some sentences begin with an **If clause** that tells a possible action. They need a clause with a resulting action to be a complete sentence. A comma separates the two clauses.

Not a Sentence	**Complete Sentence**
If you don't understand.	*If you don't understand, ask for help.*
If you tease your little brother.	*If you tease your little brother, you will get in trouble.*
If you treat others with respect.	*If you treat others with respect, they will treat you with respect.*

Finish each sentence. Be sure to write the comma where it is needed.

1. If you eat _____

2. If you open _____

3. If you help _____

4. If you read _____

5. If you tell _____

6. If you try _____

7. If you stare at _____

8. If you smile _____

Come on, Goldie!

A **declarative** sentence tells something. It ends with a period. (**.**)
An **interrogative** sentence asks something. It ends with a question mark. (**?**)
An **imperative** sentence gives an order. It ends with a period. (**.**)
An **exclamatory** sentence shows strong feeling. It ends with an exclamation mark. (**!**)

Read each sentence. Write an abbreviation to tell what kind of sentence it is:
    D—declarative   *Int*—interrogative   *Imp*—Imperative   *E*—Exclamatory
Then write the missing punctuation mark.

<u>Imp</u> Goldie, roll over**.**
<u>Int</u> Have you ever tried to train a fish**?**
<u>D</u> I did**.**
<u>E</u> What a disaster**!**

_____ 1. It all started when my friend insulted my fish
_____ 2. Fish are stupid pets
_____ 3. Why do you say that
_____ 4. Look at it
_____ 5. All your fish does is swim and eat
_____ 6. Hmmmph, Goldie is *not* a stupid fish
_____ 7. Teach her some tricks then
_____ 8. OK, I will
_____ 9. How do the trainers at Sea World train the dolphins and whales
_____ 10. They use whistles and rewards, but those are mammals, not fish
_____ 11. Goldie, swim on your side when I blow this whistle
_____ 12. Tweet-tweet
_____ 13. Goldie, didn't you hear me
_____ 14. I'll give you extra food if you do it
_____ 15. Goldie, watch how I do it

Eepee and Oogoo

Eepee and Oogoo are best friends. Choose scene A or B, and write a conversation to match. Include at least one of each of these kinds of sentences: declarative, interrogative, imperative, and exclamatory.

A. A friendly conversation

B. An argument

Eepee: _____

Oogoo: _____

Eepee: _____

Oogoo: _____

Eepee: _____

Oogoo: _____

Eepee: _____

Oogoo: _____

Animal Armor

The **subject** is the part of a sentence that tells whom or what the sentence is about. The **predicate** is the part of a sentence that tells what the subject is or does.

Read each sentence. Circle the subject. Underline the predicate.

Examples:

(Many different animals) have armor to protect themselves.
Unlike most mammals, (a pangolin) has scales covering its body.

1. The pangolin's sharp scales are made from a strange, hard form of hair.
2. A pangolin curls up in a ball to escape from danger.
3. An armadillo looks like it is covered in armor.
4. The name *armadillo* means "little armored one" in Spanish.
5. Armadillos have bony plates and very tough skin.
6. A tortoise's hard shell is its armor.
7. Inside its shell, the tortoise can hide from predators.
8. The tortoise beetle is an insect.
9. It has a hard shield that covers its head, legs, and body.

Read these animal sentences. Write **S** if the sentence is missing the subject or **P** if it is missing the predicate. Finish the sentences, filling in the missing parts.

____ 10. A slow-moving snail _____
_____.

____ 11. Like the crab, _____ is a shelled animal that lives in the ocean.

____ 12. _____ would look funny if they were covered with armor.

My Favorite Author

The **complete subject** is all the words in a sentence that tell whom or what the sentence is about.

The **simple subject** is the main word that tells whom or what the sentence is about. If a simple subject is a proper noun, it may be more than one word.

A **compound subject** has two or more simple subjects, usually connected with the word *and*.

Read each sentence. Underline the complete subject. Write the simple subject(s).

class — <u>Our class</u> is doing an author study project.

Everyone — <u>Everyone</u> needs to choose an author.

Marcus, I — <u>Both Marcus and I</u> chose Dick King-Smith.

1. Dick King-Smith writes books about animals.
2. I have read five of his books.
3. My favorite one is *Three Terrible Trins*.
4. That book is about mice triplets who befriend a cellar mouse and terrorize a cat.
5. Our assignment has two parts—a report and a project.
6. The report needs to explain themes that are repeated in the author's books.
7. Many of the characters in King-Smith's books want to do more than the others around them.
8. The mice in *Three Terrible Trins* want to have friends in all levels of their farmhouse.
9. The pig in *Pigs Might Fly* learns to swim and hopes to fly.
10. My creative project will be a tape-recorded interview of the different book characters.
11. Marcus and Whitney are going to help me read the parts.

Selling Session

The **complete predicate** is all the words in a sentence that tell what the subject is or does.

The **simple predicate** is the main verb that tells what the subject is or does. It can be more than one word.

A **compound predicate** has two or more simple predicates, connected by the words *and, but,* or *or.*

Read each sentence. Underline the complete predicate. Write the simple predicate(s).

are earning	Fifth grade students <u>are earning play money by doing jobs</u>.
hold	Our classes <u>hold a Selling Session twice a year</u>.
make, sell	We <u>make crafts and sell them to each other</u>.
_____	1. Students can buy the crafts with their play money.
_____	2. My friend Taneesha and I have three different crafts to sell.
_____	3. Taneesha spent the night at my house last Friday.
_____	4. We stayed up late and worked on our projects.
_____	5. Taneesha brought beeswax with her.
_____	6. We cut and rolled the wax to make lots of little candles.
_____	7. My mom helped us melt wax to make other candles, too.
_____	8. We carefully poured the hot wax into molds.
_____	9. Spring Break is coming soon.
_____	10. We decorated tiny flower pots with the words "Happy Spring."
_____	11. Taneesha and I made little wreaths for our last craft.
_____	12. She wrapped ribbon around each wreath.
_____	13. I glued leaves and flowers onto them.
_____	14. Selling Session will be next Friday.
_____	15. I hope lots of kids buy our crafts.

Beach Fun

Sometimes you can combine two short sentences into one longer sentence. Think about which words are repeated in the sentence as you change the wording.

Two short sentences:
 Sarah and Ian are on vacation. They are in Maine.

One longer sentence:
 Sarah and Ian are in Maine on vacation.

Read each set of sentences. Underline any words that are repeated. Look for other words that could be moved or taken out. Rewrite the set as one sentence.

1. Sarah and Ian spent the day at the beach.
 The name of the beach was Old Orchard Beach.

_____

_____

2. They looked for shells in the sand. They looked for sand dollars in the sand.

_____

_____

3. The water was cold. Sarah went body surfing in the water.

_____

_____

4. Ian waded in the waves near shore. The waves were shallow.

_____

_____

5. Ian threw seaweed at Sarah. Sarah threw seaweed at Ian.

_____

_____

6. Sarah had lots of fun that day. Ian did, too.

_____

Name _____

And...And...And...

Read the paragraph. It contains some good ideas, but the sentences are too long and rambling. Pencil in how you would change it. You may take out words, add words, or add punctuation to make the sentences sound better. Rewrite the paragraph below.

Michael Jordan is my favorite athlete and I think he is the greatest basketball player ever and maybe the greatest athlete of any sport and Michael Jordan played for the Chicago Bulls and when he was on their team, the Bulls won the NBA championship in 1991 and 1992 and 1993 and 1996 and 1997 and 1998. I think Michael is a strong, powerful player but the reason he is so good is because whenever he plays he gives his best he doesn't get lazy and not try he always tries hard and he's the greatest!

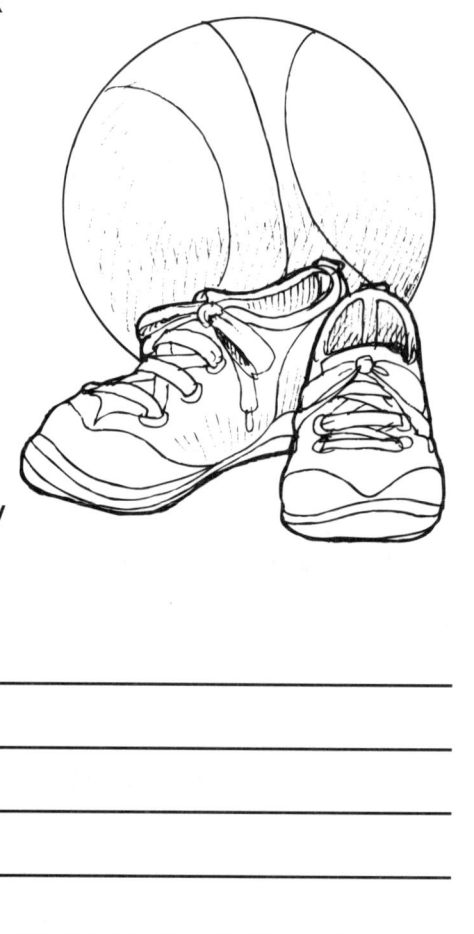

_____
_____
_____
_____
_____
_____
_____
_____
_____
_____

Name _____

Super Sentence Checklist

Use this checklist to think about the sentences you've written for stories, reports, essays, or other writing projects.

Basics

Yes   No

☐   ☐   Do your sentences begin with capital letters?

☐   ☐   Do your sentences end with the correct punctuation marks— **.** or **!** or **?**

☐   ☐   Does each sentence have a subject and a verb?

Beyond Basics

Yes   No

☐   ☐   Do your sentences vary in length—short, medium, long?

☐   ☐   Do you use a variety of sentence types—statements, questions, exclamations?

☐   ☐   Do you use creative words to help your reader picture what is being described?

☐   ☐   Do you begin your sentences in different ways?

☐   ☐   Do you use transition words to make the sentences flow? (Examples: *First, next, then, meanwhile, on the other hand, however, yet, still, in addition to, finally, lastly, in summary . . .*)

Parts of Speech

Parts of speech are categories of words. The categories are based on how words are used in a sentence. Many words can fit into more than one category. For example, *round* can be an adjective, noun, verb, adverb, or preposition. *A marble is round. We sang a round. Round these numbers to the nearest ten. Gather round. The worried parents waited round the telephone.* In English, there are eight parts of speech:

1. Nouns name a person, animal, place, thing, or idea. (*child, Fluffy, school, tree, courage*)
2. Pronouns take the place of nouns. (*they, me, hers, himself, who, those*)
3. Verbs show action or a state of being. (*scowl, flipped, am, was*)
4. Adjectives describe a noun or pronoun. (*shiny, happier, best, the*)
5. Adverbs modify a verb, an adjective, or another adverb. (*well, carefully, very*)
6. Prepositions show the position or relationship between a noun and another word. (*over, from, in spite of*)
7. Conjunctions connect words or phrases. (*and, but, or, yet, neither-nor*)
8. Interjections show emotion. (*Ouch, Yikes, Hooray*)

ABC BOOKS
Partner Activity

When studying individual parts of speech, invite pairs of students to make ABC books to match. Direct pairs to first make vertical lists of the letters of the alphabet. Have them brainstorm words next to each letter. For example, for the letter *A* in a book about prepositions, students might think of *across* and *above*. Next have students look in dictionaries, thesauruses, grammar resources, or other language books to find more words to supplement their lists. Then have each student stack four sheets of paper, fold them in half, and staple them together along the fold to make a book. Have students write the book title on the first pages, then use half pages for each letter—naming the word, using it in a sentence, and illustrating the sentence. If students cannot find a word to match a letter, have them write notes of explanation like the *Q* example on the page modeled here.

ART GALLERY
Class Activity

On a bulletin board, post a collection of prints that corresponds to an artist or period of art. (Calendars are a good resource for artwork.) Give the art space a grammar twist by displaying this question next to the prints: *What verbs does each painting make you think of?* Provide individual cards or single sheets of paper on which students may mark their responses. Change the prints and parts of speech within the question periodically to keep the activity fresh.

BLUE NOUNS

Group Activity

Review as needed that a noun names a person, animal, place, thing, or idea. Choose an adjective such as *blue*. Invite the class to think of nouns that are blue—*sky, jeans, blueberries, pen, ocean, aliens (maybe?), bruises, feathers, blue jays, bike, Violet* in *Charlie and the Chocolate Factory* by Roald Dahl (Puffin Books, 1998), *sad people*. Then let students work in small groups. One group member names an adjective. The remaining group members have one minute to name or list as many nouns as they can to match. Play until each student has had at least one turn to name the adjective.

SILENT PRACTICE

Partner Activity

Tell students that they will play this silent game with a partner. Choose a student to help you model the activity. One person thinks of a common noun category and begins to write a list of proper nouns to match. Example: *Manitoba, New Brunswick, Alberta, Ontario, Newfoundland, Prince Edward Island, British Columbia, Quebec...*(Canadian provinces) The partner may silently guess the category in writing at any time. The first player responds in writing—*yes, no,* or *be more specific*. The pair plays until the partner guesses correctly, then they switch roles. Remind students that proper nouns name specific people, places, or things, and begin with capital letters.

ABSTRACT OPPOSITES

Class Activity

Help students learn to recognize abstract nouns with this activity. Explain that concrete nouns are ones you can see, hear, smell, taste, or feel, such as *school, dad,* and *popcorn*. Abstract nouns, on the other hand, are ideas. Examples: *love, freedom, intelligence*. Brainstorm a list of abstract nouns with your students. Encourage the class to think of opposites for each to expand your list. You may want to underline suffixes found in the nouns to help students recognize those endings. Then give each student a blank sheet of paper on which to illustrate a pair of abstract noun opposites. Display the papers to share the information.

love-hate *joy-despair*
hope-hopelessness *security-insecurity*
happiness-sadness *friendship-enmity*
harmony-discord *wealth-poverty*
wisdom-foolishness *intelligence-stupidity*
justice-injustice *fear-fearlessness*

GIVE MORE DETAIL

Teach students that nouns are sometimes used within a sentence in an *appositive*, a word or phrase set off by commas that identifies or gives further details about another noun. Write these examples on the chalkboard to show how an appositive expands a sentence. Invite students to identify which noun is being described by the appositive. (speech, Craig)

Abraham Lincoln gave his most famous speech at a dedication ceremony for a Civil War cemetery.
Abraham Lincoln gave his most famous speech, the Gettysburg Address, at a dedication ceremony for a Civil War cemetery.

Ms. Walker was out of breath from racing Craig.
Ms. Walker was out of breath from racing Craig, the fastest boy in our class.

Challenge students to write three sentences of their own that contain appositives. Then let students meet with partners. Direct students to underline each appositive in their partners' sentences and to circle the nouns they describe. Follow-up the activity by having students look for appositives in both fiction and nonfiction books.

HOW MANY?

Review with students that a singular noun names one person, place, thing, or idea and a plural noun names more than one. Ask students what letter is added to the ends of most singular nouns to make them plural. (s) Give pairs of students copies of the activity sheet *Star-Stars* (page 32) to complete. It introduces spelling patterns to help students form plural nouns. After students have finished the page, hold a class discussion to compare results. Then ask students what they could do if they were not sure how to spell the plural form of a noun. (Ideas: ask someone else, try the spell check on a computer, look up the word in a dictionary)

VOLCANOS? VOLCANOES?

Many nouns that end in *o* are made plural by adding *s*: *cello-cellos, zoo-zoos*. Others are made plural by adding *es*: *hero-heroes, potato-potatoes*. Some are correct either way: *volcano-volcanos-volcanoes, zero-zeros-zeroes*. Model for students how to find a noun's plural form in the dictionary. (Some give the plural form of every noun; others give irregular plurals only.) Then tell students to choose 10 of these tricky words, to look them up in the dictionary, and to write their plural forms: *banjo, radio, tomato, mosquito, piano, stereo, veto, domino, rodeo, echo, halo, torpedo, photo, lasso, motto, solo*.

A SWARM OF BEES

Class Activity

Read aloud Ruth Heller's delightful book *A Cache of Jewels and Other Collective Nouns* (Grosset & Dunlap, 1987). Then challenge students to make their own lists of collective nouns that describe animals (herd, gaggle, pod . . .). Discuss possible resources for finding those nouns—nature magazines, animal books, dictionaries, and encyclopedias. Encourage creative word use in stories by inviting children to describe groupings with unusual collective nouns. Example: *A swarm of kindergartners surrounded the clown.*

WHOSE ARE THEY?

Class Activity

Before the lesson, write on separate pieces of tagboard the letter *s*, an apostrophe, and these words: *boy, boys, girl, girls, baby, babies, child, children, woman, women, man, men, the,* and *books*. At the chalkboard, teach or review how to use an apostrophe to show possession.

- an apostrophe s ('s) is added to the end of singular nouns (*boy—the boy's pencils*)
- an apostrophe (') is added to the end of plural nouns that end with s (*girls—the girls' pencils*)
- an apostrophe s ('s) is added to the end of plural nouns that do not end with s (*children—the children's pencils*)

Then invite three students to come to the front of the class, hand them some books, and have them pretend to be babies reading. Tell the class these books belong to the babies. Model how to arrange the tagboard signs on the chalkboard shelf to make the matching possessive phrase: *the babies' books*. Repeat the activity several times, calling on different students to act out different parts while another student creates the matching possessive phrase. Direct students at their desks to write the phrase and then compare their answers to the tagboard version.

TITLE SORT

Partner Activity

Singular common nouns	Plural common nouns
song homecoming web trumpet swan house prairie paint	shores woods
Proper nouns Stuart Little Silver Lake Danny Dunn	**Possessive nouns** Dicey's Charlotte's

Do this activity in the library. Have pairs of students each choose a shelf in the fiction section. Direct partners to read through the titles on their shelves, looking for nouns. Have students record their findings on sheets of paper divided into fourths and labeled with these headings: *singular common nouns, plural common nouns, proper nouns,* and *possessive nouns*. Tell students to classify the nouns by what types they were before they became part of the title.

REUSE THEM!
Partner Activity

Don't just recycle old notices and newsletters, reuse them! For an ongoing activity, have student pairs skim through old notices and circle all the pronouns they find. Direct them to write in the margins the nouns the pronouns replace. Call on several students to read aloud sentences and explain what they marked. As students begin to expand their knowledge of pronouns, the amount of pronouns circled should increase.

WORD PROBLEMS
Group Activity

Use math word problems to teach a mini-lesson on subject pronouns and object pronouns. Explain that a subject pronoun can take the place of a noun in the subject of a sentence. An object pronoun takes the place of a noun that receives the action of a verb or follows a preposition. Call on different students to read aloud a word problem, identify the pronouns, tell what nouns they take the place of, and explain why the pronoun used was a subject pronoun or an object pronoun. Then let groups of students write 3-10 word problems of their own, using all 14 pronouns in the chart. Tell students to make sure they use the pronouns *you* and *it* both as subject pronouns and object pronouns.

Subject Pronouns	Object Pronouns
I	me
you	you
he	him
she	her
it	it
we	us
they	them

WHOSE BODY?
Class Activity

I used a stuffed animal's head, a man's body, and two kids' legs.

I used its head, his body, and their legs.

Let students mix and match body parts for some silly pronoun practice. Gather ready-to-be-recycled catalogs, nature magazines, and newspaper inserts. Direct students to cut apart different pictures, mix and match the body parts, and glue them to another sheet of paper to make a new creature. Then have students write two sentences that explain whose body parts were used. The first sentence should use possessive nouns and the second should repeat the same information using possessive pronouns.

ANYONE, NO ONE, SOMEONE, EVERYONE
Class Activity

Indefinite pronouns replace nouns in a general, indefinite way. Challenge students to combine *any, some, no, every, body, one,* and *thing* to make 12 different indefinite pronouns. Then brainstorm other indefinite pronouns, such as these: *each, few, both, many, most, some, none, neither, either, several, others.*

SKETCH IT!

Partner Activity

Review with students that most verbs are action words. Challenge pairs of students to sketch verb pictures, like the samples here, that show the words and their meanings. Suggest that students brainstorm lists of 20 or more verbs and from that choose 10 to illustrate. Post the grammar artwork on a wall or bulletin board to let students see their classmates' creations.

VERB OF THE DAY

Class Activity

Tell students that using precise action verbs can spruce up writing, as shown in the example below. *Growled* gives the reader a better picture of the toddler than *said* does.

"I don't want to do that," said the toddler.
"I don't want to do that," growled the toddler.

Teach students how to use a thesaurus to find alternative verbs. Then give students the responsibility of learning and teaching new vocabulary. Assign each student a different day. For homework leading up to that day, the student must find a verb in a thesaurus or dictionary that he or she did not know before. Provide five minutes in your schedule for "Verb of the Day" time. The featured student should write the word on a cumulative class chart, explain its meaning and how it differs from similar verbs, and use it in a sentence. Encourage students to use these new verbs from the class chart in their own writing.

HELP!

Group Activity

Teach or review that some verbs are helping verbs—they help action verbs within a sentence. Post a chart of these helping verbs. Explain that a sentence may have one, two or three helping verbs along with an action verb. Examples:

Have you (chosen) a project yet?
No, I *will* (choose) my project soon.
Ellen *has been* (making) origami animals.
I *could have been* (done) by now if I *had* (started) earlier.

Helping Verbs

am, is, are, was, were, be, being, been

do, does, did

have, has, had

can, could, should, would

may, might, must

will, shall

Invite students to work with partners or in small groups. Direct students to hunt through books or magazines to find 10 sentences with helping verbs. Have them copy the sentences, underline the helping verbs, and circle the action verbs that are being "helped."

FS123304 Grammar Made Simple Grade 5 ■ © Frank Schaffer Publications, Inc.

Homework

Today Is (Bzzz) Going...

The verb *be* in all its forms *(am, is, are, was, were, be, been, being)* is the most common verb in the English language. It can be a linking verb or a helping verb. As a linking verb, it is followed by an adjective or noun that describes the subject. As a helping verb, it helps show the tense of action verbs. Challenge students to informally determine if *be* truly is the most common verb. Have them quietly make a buzzer sound *(bzzz)* whenever they hear any form of the word *be*. Direct them to do the activity *outside* of school for one hour. If students watch TV at home, suggest they try listening for *be* words for 15 minutes with their eyes closed.

Be as a *linking verb:*
  I am *hungry.*
  My dad was a *pilot in the Gulf War.*

Be as a *helping verb:*
  Are *you taking the bus downtown?*
  Our class has been *studying U.S. presidents.*

Be as *both:*
  We were being *silly!*

TAKE-TOOK, BAKE-BOOK?

Class Activity

Teach students these rules for changing present tense verbs to past tense:

1. For most verbs, add *ed* to the present tense form. Examples: *play-played, answer-answered*

2. For verbs ending in *e*, drop the *e* and add *ed*. Examples: *dribble-dribbled, type-typed*

3. For verbs ending in consonant-*y*, change the *y* to *i* and add *ed*.
   Examples: *cry-cried, study-studied*

4. Some verbs are irregular. Examples: *think-thought, go-went*

Challenge students to list rhyming present-tense verb pairs whose past tense forms don't rhyme. Give them this frame to recite when testing words.

(Verb)   Today I think. Yesterday I thought.
(Rhyming verb)   Today I wink. Yesterday I wought?

snow-snowed grow-growed?
give-gave live-lave?
tell-told smell-smold?
cry-cried fly-flied?
write-wrote bite-bote?
know-knew show-shew?
free-freed see-seed?

AWESOME! GROSS! WEIRD!

Partner Activity

Invite students to bring in catalogs of items that interest them—toys, clothes, sports equipment, craft materials, and so on. Let students work with partners. Challenge each pair to choose a catalog, to skim through it, and to list 100 *different* adjectives to describe items within it. Have students mark the words they've used with pens, right on the catalog pages, numbering their adjective lists as they go along.

I SPY

Partner Activity

Let students play this game with partners, either as an oral activity or a silent writing activity. One partner picks an item in the room visible to both players. That person says (or writes), "I spy with my little eye something that is . . . " and then lists seven adjectives that describe the item. The other player guesses the item. If the player makes an incorrect guess, the first player responds with a clue that involves one or more adjectives telling why the guess is wrong. Example: *No, a ruler is long and thin. My item is not long and thin.* The game continues until the partner guesses correctly. Then players switch roles.

SMELLY, SMELLIER, SMELLIEST

Group Activity

Connect science observations with grammar in this activity. First teach or review that adjectives that compare two items end with *er* or use the words *more* or *less*, while adjectives that compare more than two items end with *est* or use the words *most* or *least*. Then have students work in groups of three. Direct each student within the group to choose an item he or she is studying and list five adjectives that describe it. (Examples: If you are studying the solar system, each person might describe a different planet. If you are studying marine biology, each person might describe an animal that lives in the sea.) Next have students write 10 sentences that compare the items in their groups using the adjectives. Direct students to vary the forms of the adjectives they use—positive, comparative, and superlative.

Positive (describes one)	Comparative (compares two)	Superlative (compares more than two)
big	bigger	biggest
dangerous	more dangerous less dangerous	most dangerous least dangerous

1. Marisa's bean seeds are smelly.
2. Frankie's seeds are even smellier.
3. Anne Marie's seeds that were watered with milk are the smelliest.
4.
5.
6.
7.
8.
9.
10.

PIPE-CLEANER PEOPLE — Class Activity

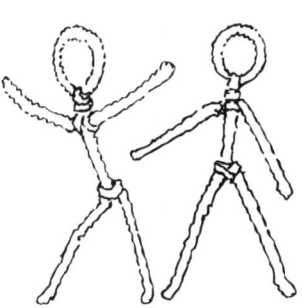

Give each student one pipe cleaner with the direction to transform it into an original pipe-cleaner person. Next ask for a volunteer to give you an action verb, such as *swim*, that tells what the pipe-cleaner person can do. Challenge students to make their pipe-cleaner people act out *how* it does that verb—gracefully, fast, slowly, and so on. Invite students to write those words on the chalkboard. Explain that they are adverbs, words that modify a verb. Continue the activity until most or all students have had a chance to name a verb or adverb.

HOW? WHEN? WHERE? — Class Activity

Teach students that adverbs answer these questions: How, When, and Where? Write this simple sentence on the chalkboard: *I play the guitar.* Direct the students to copy the sentence at their desks and to add an adverb that tells *how* you play the guitar. (*well, badly, expertly, skillfully, quietly, seriously*) Invite students to read aloud their sentences. Create a list of their adverbs on the chalkboard under the heading *How?* Next tell them to add one word that tells *when* you play the guitar. (*Monday, sometimes, never, always, everyday*) Again have students read aloud their sentences, and list their adverbs under the heading *When?* Then tell students to add one word that tells *where* you play the guitar. (*indoors, outside, here, there, everywhere, nearby*) Have students read aloud their sentences, and list their adverbs under the heading *Where?* For a follow-up homework assignment, have each student skim through a chapter in a book and copy five sentences that have adverbs in them.

You may want to use this lesson to point out that a word can be more than one part of speech, depending on how it is used in a sentence. *Monday I play the guitar.* (*Monday* is used as an adverb.) *Monday is my favorite day.* (*Monday* is used as a noun.)

NOT, VERY, TOO — Partner Activity

Explain that the three most common adverbs in English are *not, very,* and *too.* Challenge pairs of students to write sentences using these adverbs in three different ways—to modify a verb, to modify an adjective, and to modify another adverb. Examples: *You may not drive. He is not sleepy. She is not very generous.* (*Very* can modify an adjective or adverb, but not a verb.)

FOUND IN A PHRASE — Group Activity

In fancy clothes, behind the door, two mice are dancing on the floor.

If your students are unfamiliar with prepositions, read aloud Ruth Heller's book *Behind the Mask* (Grosset & Dunlap, 1995). It uses rhyming verse to introduce prepositions, which are always found in phrases. Then let students work in small groups to write and illustrate rhyming verses that include prepositions.

NEVER END A SENTENCE WITH . . .   *Class Activity*

One of the rules you may remember from when you learned grammar is "Never end a sentence with a preposition." Use this rule as an opportunity to teach how spoken language is sometimes different from written language. For example, if a child were to say, "I'm going to the county fair," her friend might ask, "Who are you going with?" If written formally, that question would be, "With whom are you going?" Here is a general guideline you may want to give your students: Try to avoid ending a sentence with a preposition in writing; but if it sounds too awkward, leave the preposition at the end.

CONNECT IT!   *Partner Activity*

> *I like to eat warm and chewy chocolate chip cookies.*
> *Andre and James are coming over today.*
> *Karina likes to watch the monkeys climb and swing.*
> *My dad sings passionately and terribly.*
> *We played in and around the trees.*
> *You and I should work together on the diorama project.*

Conjunctions are connecting words. *And* is the most common conjunction. It can connect nouns, pronouns, verbs, adjectives, adverbs, and prepositions, as well as phrases and sentences. Challenge students to write their own sentences that show *and* connecting those six different parts of speech. Then have them trade papers with partners to determine what *and* is connecting in each sentence.

PAIR UP!   *Class Activity*

Explain that some conjunctions come in pairs—both/and, either/or, neither/nor, not only/but also, whether/or. Invite students to imagine a very strict teacher and write (or tell) sentences he or she might utter using these conjunction pairs. Examples: <u>Both</u> *Matthew* <u>and</u> *Minerva will stay after school today and write 1,000 times "I will not breathe loudly in class."* <u>Not only</u> *shall everyone memorize the names of the vice-presidents in chronological order, but also the places and years they were born.*

YOU ARE LOST IN SPACE—WAAAGH!   *Partner Activity*

Teach or review that interjections are words or phrases that show emotions or strong feelings—*Hey! Watch out! Eek!* Interjections are usually found at the beginnings of sentences: *Ouch, that hurt!* not *That hurt, ouch!* Let students work with partners for this activity. One person names a situation and the partner gives a matching interjection. Direct students to switch roles and continue the activity for three minutes, thinking of a new interjection each time they switch. End by having partners write their favorite interjections.

FS123304 Grammar Made Simple Grade 5 • © Frank Schaffer Publications, Inc.

Name_____

The Noun Category Game

A **noun** names a person, animal, place, thing, or idea.

Play this game with a partner. Each of you needs your own paper. Together choose two more letters and two more noun categories, and write them in the heading boxes. For five minutes, write as many nouns as you can that match each category and begin with the given letter. Example: B animal—*bat.* You get one point for each word. The player with the most points wins.

Letters

Categories	B	S		
Animal				
Food				

Noun Analogies

An **analogy** shows a pattern between words. The analogy below is read *horse is to foal as cow is to _____*. To think of the missing word, you need to recognize that the pattern is the name of an adult animal and the name of its young. The missing word would be *calf*.

horse : foal :: cow : _____

Read these analogies. Write the missing noun. Here are some patterns you may find:
synonyms
antonyms
singular-plural
common-proper nouns
part-whole
purpose

1. Monday : day :: February : _____
2. sheep : flock :: fish : _____
3. girl : girls :: woman : _____
4. star : Sun :: planet : _____
5. elf : elves :: wolf : _____
6. selfishness : generosity :: cruelty : _____
7. ruler : length :: thermometer : _____
8. burger : hamburger :: phone : _____
9. dictionary : words :: atlas : _____
10. morning : dawn :: evening : _____
11. state : California :: city : _____
12. person : people :: child : _____
13. mammal : elephant :: reptile : _____
14. England : English :: Japan : _____
15. foot : feet :: tooth : _____
16. hope : despair :: wisdom : _____
17. cactus : cacti :: octopus : _____
18. win : victory :: loss : _____
19. ocean : Atlantic :: river : _____
20. Canada : Canadian :: Mexico : _____

Name _____

Star-Stars

A **singular noun** names one person, place, thing, or idea.
A **plural noun** names more than one.

Read the spelling rules and examples.
Write your own singular and plural noun pairs to match each rule.

Rule	Examples	How many noun pairs can you write that match the rule?
1. Most nouns are made plural by adding **s**.	star-stars house-houses	
2. Nouns that end with an **s, ch, sh, x,** or **z** are made plural by adding **es**.	kiss-kisses peach-peaches box-boxes	
3. Nouns that end with a vowel-**y** are made plural by adding **s**. Nouns that end with a consonant-**y** are made plural by changing the **y** to **i** and adding **es**.	boy-boys essay-essays sky-skies library-libraries	
4. Many nouns that end with an **f** or **fe** are made plural by changing the **f** to **v** and adding **es**.	shelf-shelves wife-wives	
5. Some nouns have irregular plurals. Many of them name animals.	child-children foot-feet mouse-mice sheep-sheep	

A Thank-You Note

A. Read Liz Beth's letter to her grandparents.
   Fill in the missing subject pronouns.

B. Read her grandpa's reply.
   Fill in the missing object pronouns.

C. Compare answers with a partner.
   Take turns naming the noun each pronoun replaces.

Subject Pronoun	Object Pronoun
I	me
you	you
he	him
she	her
it	it
we	us
they	them

Dear Grandma and Grandpa,

　　Thank you for the earrings _____ sent me for my birthday. _____ were cool. Dad still thinks ___ am too young to have had my ears pierced. But he said now that _____ is done, he won't complain about it anymore. Last night Michael asked Dad if _____ could get one of his ears pierced. Dad got really mad and said, "___ am going for a long walk!" _____ all started laughing. Mom doesn't think Michael really wants his ear pierced. _____ thinks he just wanted to tease Dad.

　　_____ are looking forward to your visit next month. _____ is coming soon. If _____ have time, please write me back.

　　　　　　　　　　Love,
　　　　　　　　　　Liz Beth

Dear Liz Beth,

　　We were so happy to get the note you sent _____. Grandma picked out the earrings. We're glad you liked _____. Your poor father—you three are always picking on _____!

　　Grandma is at Aunt Yoli's this weekend. She went to visit _____ for a few days.

　　I talked to your mom yesterday. She told _____ that you won a mystery award for your computer project. When will you get _____?

　　I hope all is well with you and your family. We miss _____.

　　　　　　　　　　Love,
　　　　　　　　　　Grandpa

Pronoun Power

For each theme, choose a different row of pronouns from the chart. Write a set of sentences that uses each pronoun in a row and matches the given theme.

Subject Pronoun	Object Pronoun	Possessive Pronouns	
I	me	my	mine
you	you	your	yours
he	him	his	his
she	her	her	hers
we	us	our	ours
they	them	their	theirs

Sample

trees — *Do you know that tree? It is following you. How did it get out of your yard? Is that weird tree yours?*

pets

sports

famous places

Name_____

Score Four—A Verb Game

Play this game with a partner. Take turns choosing a box and completing the activity. If your partner agrees you did it correctly, you can shade in the box with the crayon color of your choice.

The winner is the first player to have four boxes in a row—horizontally ▭▭▭▭, vertically ▯, diagonally ▱▱▱▱, or a box of four ▤.

Use *was* as a helping verb in a sentence with another verb.	Name two synonyms for the verb *think*.	Use the past tense of *play* in a sentence.	Name five verbs that match what an artist might do.	Use *do* as a helping verb in a command that contains another verb.
What do you like to do for fun? List 10 action verbs.	Use each of the helping verbs *should, would,* and *could* in its own sentence.	Name three antonyms for *laugh*.	Use *were* in a question.	Give a sentence that contains four verbs.
Use *bring* and *brought* in their own sentences.	What are five verbs you could use in place of *said*?	What do frogs do that you do not? List six action verbs.	Use each of the "be" verbs, *am, is,* and *are*, in its own sentence.	Name three synonyms for the verb *run*.
Name three antonyms for *hate*.	Use *have* and *been* as helping verbs in a sentence with another verb.	Use one of these linking verbs in a sentence: *seem, appear,* or *feel*.	Use *sing* and *sang* in their own sentences.	What do scientists do? List 10 action verbs.
Use each of the helping verbs *may, must,* and *might* in its own sentence.	Name three synonyms for *wash*.	Give two future tense sentences that use the helping verb *will*.	Use *being* in a sentence with another verb.	Use *ride, rode,* and *ridden* in their own sentences.

FS123304 Grammar Made Simple Grade 5 ■ © Frank Schaffer Publications, Inc.

reproducible

Name _____

A Bad Fairy Tale

Most verbs name actions. The verb **be** is different. It tells about someone or something. It can also be a helping verb that helps with an action verb.

Read this silly fairy tale. Fill in the blanks with a form of the verb **be**: *be, am, is, are, was, were, being,* or *been*.

Once upon a time, there _____ a sweet, unlucky girl named Mary Badluck. Like other mothers in fairy tales, her mother _____ gentle, kind, and ill. Unfortunately, Mary's mother died when Mary _____ only five. Mary and her father _____ quite sad. "What _____ we going to do?" wept her father.

"I _____ not worried, Father, nor should you be," said Mary. "We will _____ okay."

Mary's father _____ lonely, so he remarried. Mary's stepmother, Lady Grace, _____ gentle and kind like Mary's own mother had _____. But alas, Lady Grace _____ ill, too, and she soon died.

"What _____ I going to do?" sobbed her father.

"_____ brave, Father!" admonished Mary.

Once again her father remarried. Mary's new stepmother, Lady Evila, _____ actually nice. Mary had _____ expecting an evil stepmother and _____ pleasantly surprised. But guess what? Yes, you _____ right. Lady Evila _____ a sickly creature and died, too.

"What _____ going on around here?" wailed her father.

"I think we are _____ tormented in a bad fairy tale, Father!" realized Mary.

Mary _____ quite right. Her father remarried yet again. This time her new stepmother, Lady Bullybrains, _____ rough, mean, and healthy.

What _____ Mary and her father going to do? Will they ever _____ happy? Write an ending to this tale to find out.

Name _____

Begin, Began, Begun

Most verbs are made past tense by adding *ed*.
But many verbs, such as *begin*, are **irregular**.

Today I <u>begin</u> my flute lessons.
Yesterday I <u>began</u> my flute lessons.
I had already <u>begun</u> my flute lessons.

Fill in the missing verbs in this chart of irregular past tense verbs.

Present Tense	Past Tense	Past Participle (use with *has, have,* or *had*)	Present Tense	Past Tense	Past Participle (use with *has, have,* or *had*)
begin	began	begun	give		given
bite	bit	bitten	go	went	
	broke	broken		grew	grown
bring		brought	hide		hidden
buy	bought		know	knew	
	chose	chosen		saw	seen
come		come	sing		sung
do	did		speak	spoke	
	drew	drawn		stood	stood
drink		drunk	swim		swum
drive	drove		take	took	
	ate	eaten		thought	thought
fall		fallen	throw		thrown
fly	flew		wear	wore	
	got	gotten		wrote	written

What Am I Describing?

An **adjective** is a word that describes a person, place, or thing.

1. Choose two items from the list to compare and contrast in each Venn diagram.
2. In the space where the ovals overlap, write adjectives that describe both items.
3. In the remaining space in each oval, write adjectives that describe only that item.
4. Don't label the ovals. Challenge a partner to read each diagram and figure out which two items you described.

Can you figure out which two items were described in this sample?

Item List
- a cactus
- a cat
- a dinosaur
- a dog
- a doughnut
- spaghetti
- yarn
- you
- your best friend

Sample Venn diagram:
- Left oval only: agile, independent, sleepy, soft
- Overlap: furry, four-legged, alive
- Right oval only: friendly, slobbery, trainable, loyal

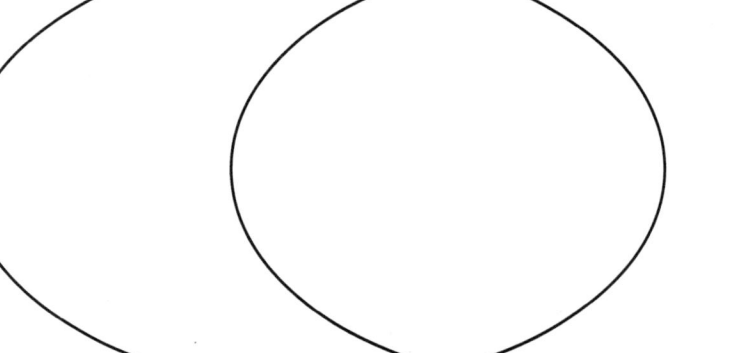

Name _____

Noun, Adjective, Adverb

A **noun** is a word that names a person, place, thing, or idea.
An **adjective** is a word that describes a noun.
An **adverb** is a word that modifies a verb, an adjective, or another adverb.

Many nouns, adjectives, and adverbs are variations of the same root word.
  <u>Bravery</u> was an important quality for knights. (noun)
  The <u>brave</u> knight searched for the dragon. (adjective)
  The knight fought <u>bravely</u> when the dragon attacked. (adverb)

Read the words in each row. Write the missing adjective or adverb.

Noun	Adjective	Adverb
intelligence	intelligent	intelligently
kindness		kindly
fearlessness	fearless	
happiness		happily
success		successfully
independence		
arrogance	arrogant	
carelessness		carelessly
possibility		
enthusiasm		enthusiastically
affection	affectionate	
ease		
courtesy		courteously
responsibility		responsibly
stupidity		
wisdom		
anger		
silence		

How? When? Where?

An **adverb** is a word that modifies a verb. Adverbs may tell how something is done (*slowly, angrily*), when it is done (*later, never*), or where it is done (*here, inside*).

Read each sentence. Underline the adverb.
Write the question it answers: *How?*, *When?*, or *Where?*

When?	The fifth grade Outdoor Education trip ends <u>tomorrow</u>.
_____	1. The week went by quickly.
_____	2. Some of the kids had never been to the mountains.
_____	3. Most of the lessons were held outdoors.
_____	4. A typical day began early with a 7 a.m. breakfast.
_____	5. The fifth graders hiked endlessly.
_____	6. Along the way, they carefully searched for animal tracks.
_____	7. The students rarely found tracks.
_____	8. But they found bugs everywhere!
_____	9. A few bugs bit children unmercifully.
_____	10. The students had many things to do outside.
_____	11. Some of the kids bravely tackled the ropes course.
_____	12. Others went swimming, cautiously entering the chilly water.
_____	13. A few kids read peacefully beside a tree.
_____	14. Later everyone would meet in the Main Hall.
_____	15. Groups energetically performed silly skits about the environment.
_____	16. The audience would groan and applaud loudly.
_____	17. Then all the exhausted kids went to bed.

Put Them Together

A **conjunction** is a connecting word. It can connect words, phrases, or sentences.

Mr. Rivera is a great teacher. I think he gives too much homework.
Mr. Rivera is a great teacher, <u>but</u> I think he gives too much homework.

Each sentence in the left column could be combined with a sentence in the right column to make a longer compound sentence. Draw lines to match up the sentences. On the line, write the conjunction you would use to connect the sentences: *and, or, but, for,* or *yet.*

I think your hair looks cool.	I might just stay home and relax.
I earned $10 doing extra chores.	It would look better if you hadn't dyed it green.
I might go to day camp this summer.	I can't play this song well.
I've been studying harder.	Now I have enough money to buy a skateboard.
I keep practicing the flute.	I may use it to build a fort.
I picked blueberries at my grandpa's.	I'll be grounded if I don't get better grades.
I may use the wood to build a treehouse.	I'll use them when I bake muffins.

Choose two of the sets above to write as compound sentences. Be sure to write a comma before the conjunction.

_____
_____
_____
_____

Usage

Usage is how we use language effectively and appropriately. Although various communities have their own patterns for informal speech, it is important that all students learn to speak and write standard English. Standard English is the language of educated people. Many people judge others by the way they speak. What would your initial reaction be to someone who said, "He don't know nothing"? Children need to repeatedly hear language spoken correctly in order for it to become natural in their own speech and writing. Therefore, you should strive to include oral practice of correct forms whenever possible in your usage lessons.

GOOFY GRAMMAR SAYS . . .
Class Activity

As you teach lessons on usage, let students apply what they've learned by creating Goofy Grammar cartoons. Tell each student to fold a sheet of blank paper in half. On one half, he or she creates a cartoon titled "Goofy Grammar says . . ." with a goofy-looking character saying an incorrect sentence. On the other half, each student creates a cartoon titled "One should say . . ." with a "cool-looking" character saying the correct version of the sentence. Have students compile their cartoons into their own personal usage books.

SLOPPY SPEECH
Class Activity

Sloppy Speech
wanna—want to
gonna—going to
gotta—got to
shoulda—should have
woulda—would have
coulda—could have
gimme—give me
sorta—sort of
kinda—kind of
watcha—what are you
         what do you
wadtcha—what did you

Write these words on a chart labeled "Sloppy Speech": *wanna, gonna, gotta, shoulda, woulda, coulda, gimme, sorta, kinda, watcha, wadtcha.* Ask a volunteer to use *wanna* in a sentence and tell what it means. (*I wanna go home. want to*) Next to *wanna*, write the precise words it stands for. Tell students you don't *want to* hear sloppy speech in your class. Challenge each person in the class to give a sentence using *want to*. Continue through the list to help students hear and see the precise words each sloppy term stands for. Leave the chart on the wall as a reminder for students.

UNDER THREE MINUTES — Class Activity

Here's a quick and easy activity to do while waiting in line or filling other spare moments. Invite a student to name a verb—for example, *snowboard*. Briskly go through the class, having each student name a different subject followed by the correct present tense form of the verb. (*I snowboard. Eric snowboards. My little sister Jocelyn snowboards. They snowboard. No one I know snowboards. Both of them snowboard.*) If a student misuses the verb, make a simple buzzer sound and return to that student when all others have had their first turn. Set a time frame within which the entire class will answer, such as three minutes.

CROSSWORD PUZZLE PRACTICE — Partner Activity

Give each student a copy of the reproducible *Singular or Plural?* (page 50). The page is a resource on collective nouns and indefinite pronouns to help students with subject/verb agreement. Take time to read through the page as a class and to discuss the examples. Then have students work with partners to create crossword puzzles that feature some of the words. Here are steps for students to follow:

1. Choose 12 words from the page, including at least one from each category.
2. Arrange the words on graph paper to make a crossword puzzle.
3. Trace a blank grid for your puzzle. Number the first box in each word.
4. Write a present-tense sentence clue for each word that has a blank for the noun or pronoun. Example: The fifth-grade ____ is performing a concert this week.
5. Try out your puzzle, reading each clue and lightly writing its answer in pencil. Make corrections as needed. Erase the answers.
6. Exchange and solve puzzles with another pair of students.

I SAY, OL' CHAP . . . — Group Activity

Direct students to work in groups of four for this oral language activity. Each group will need a completed version of the page 37 reproducible *Begin, Began, Begun*. Give students these directions: The first person in the group chooses an accent (British, French, Southern drawl, New Jersey . . .), the second person chooses a past tense or past participle verb from the page, the third uses the verb in a sentence speaking with an accent, and the fourth person determines whether or not the verb was used correctly. Tell students to rotate roles each round. Explain that a person can deliberately misuse a verb to see if the others will catch the mistake. Let groups play several rounds to give them practice using the verbs and listening for them.

COMMON MIX-UPS

Class Activity

Many pairs of words confuse students (and adults). Do this activity to practice the usage of words that your students mix up. Follow these steps for each pair.

1. Explain the meaning of each word in the pair. (See sample explanations.)

2. Use the words in sample sentences.

3. Write a sample sentence for each word with a blank where the word will go. Invite the class to call out the correct word. Ask a student to explain why the answer is correct or not.

4. Challenge students to write their own sentences for each word with blanks where the words will go. Collect the sentences.

5. Give each student an index card. He or she will write one word on the front side and the other on the back.

6. Read aloud the student-written sentences. Have students hold up the cards showing you the correct words for the sentences.

7. Save the sentences to use as review throughout the year. Have students store their index cards in envelopes at their desks.

can/may—*can* means "able to"; *may* means "permitted to"

teach/learn—*teach* means "give information"; *learn* means "get information"

of/have—*of* is a preposition and is usually followed (not necessarily directly) by a noun or pronoun; *have* is an action verb or a helping verb

then/than—*then* tells when; *than* compares

between/among—*between* is used when speaking of two persons or things; *among* is used when speaking of more than two

good/well—*good* is an adjective that describes a noun; *well* is usually an adverb that describes how something is done; it can also be an adjective meaning "healthy"

ME AND . . .

Partner Activity

Even in fifth grade, many children still begin a sentence with "*Me and ___ . . .*" rather than "*___ and I . . .*" Review with students that the speaker should always name himself or herself last. Challenge pairs to make up rhymes to review this important concept. Let students post their best rhymes on the wall. Whenever you hear a student name himself or herself first (*Me and Danielle don't understand what . . .*), have that student or the entire class recite one of the rhymes as a reminder.

Say "blank and I," not "Me and blank," or Mrs. Knox will be a crank!

Hey, watch it, dude. Don't be so rude. Make your buddy number one, And then your turn will come.

HE, SHE, HIM, HER, THEY, THEM

Group Activity

Choosing whether to use a subject pronoun or an object pronoun is a problem for many students. Do this activity to give them practice writing, reading, speaking, and listening to a variety of sentences using pronouns. First give students the general guidelines shown in the box. Then have them work in groups to follow these steps:

1. Choose and cut out three pictures from a magazine—one of a girl or woman, one of a boy or man, and one of two people (male or female). Tape or glue each picture to the center of a large sheet of paper.

2. Make up a name for each person and write a sentence above the picture that follows this frame: *Meet _____.*

> Use a subject pronoun (*I, you, he, she, it, we, they*) when . . .
> - the pronoun is the subject of a sentence or clause
>   <u>He</u> said Aunt Ellen would come at 2:00.
>   <u>They</u> were worried when <u>she</u> didn't come.
> - or the pronoun follows a form of the verb *be* and renames the subject.
>   Who is it? It is <u>I</u>.
>
> Use an object pronoun (*me, you, him, her, it, us, them*) when . . .
> - the pronoun directly receives the action of a verb
>   Aunt Ellen called <u>them</u> later.
> - the pronoun indirectly receives the action of a verb
>   Aunt Ellen sent <u>us</u> flowers.
> - or the pronoun is the object of a preposition.
>   Uncle Charlie took a picture of <u>her</u>.

Meet Dagwood and Donella.

Miguel lives next door to them.

You may have seen them on TV.

They are amazing.

All the local news stations interviewed them.

They invented a new kind of bubble gum.

Next year they will both compete in the Olympics in the diving competition.

3. In the space surrounding the picture, write six sentences about the person (or people). Each sentence should use a pronoun rather than the person's name. Vary the sentences so that three include subject pronouns (*he, she*, or *they*) and the other three include object pronouns (*him, her,* or *them*).

4. Have your sentences checked to make sure they are correct.

5. As a group, show your pictures to the class and read aloud the matching sentences.

WHO OR WHOM?

Class Activity

Once your students have mastered *she vs. her* or *he vs. him*, they should be ready to tackle *who vs. whom*. Although *who* is often acceptable in casual speech in place of *whom*, it is still important to teach children the correct use of this relative pronoun. The simplest way to do so is to think of the difference between the pronouns *he* and *him*. Like *he*, *who* is a subject pronoun. Like *him*, *whom* is an object pronoun.

> Who is the leader of your writing team? He is the leader.
> Whom did you give your form to? (or To whom did you give your form?) I gave him my form.

Direct students to go back to their pictures from the idea above and make up a question correctly using *who* or *whom* for each sentence. Example: Who is amazing? Whom did the local news stations interview?

TWO NEGATIVES = A POSITIVE

Partner Activity

If your math curriculum includes teaching negative numbers, you may want to schedule your grammar lesson on double negatives at the same time. Write this sentence on the chalkboard: *You don't know nothing.* Ask students if they can identify the negative (or no) words in the sentence. (*not* in the contraction *don't, nothing*) Explain that in a sentence with two negatives, the negatives cancel each other out. Therefore, "you don't know nothing" means "you do know something." So, if the intent is to be negative, the sentence should have just one negative word. Correct versions: *You know nothing. You don't know anything.* (Exception: The conjunction pair *Neither/nor* count as one negative. *Neither you nor your friend knows anything.*)

Together, brainstorm a list of negative words on the chalkboard, including any contractions you can think of with *n't*. (See page 53 for suggestions.) Then let students practice the lesson with partners. One partner gives a double negative sentence. The other partner replies with "No, no, no!" followed by the correct negative sentence. Let students switch roles and repeat the activity for several rounds. Encourage students to think of both statements and questions.

A BRAGGING CONTEST

Class Activity

Adjective	Comparing two	Comparing more than two
smart	smarter	smartest
generous	more generous	most generous
good	better	best
bad	worse	worst

Adverb	Comparing two	Comparing more than two
fast	faster	fastest
softly	more softly	most softly
well	better	best
badly	worse	worst

Review with students how adjectives and adverbs change form when they are comparing two items and more than two. Then tell students you want to have a bragging contest. Invite students to write two boastful (and not necessarily truthful) statements about themselves. Specify that one sentence should use an adjective in its basic form and the other should use an adverb in its basic form. Call on a volunteer to stand and proudly give his or her boast. Next outdo that student's boast, using the comparative form of the adjective or adverb. Then ask for another volunteer to end the round of boasting with a superlative adjective or adverb. Continue until all students have had at least one chance to brag. If a student should incorrectly use an adjective or adverb, guide the student in correcting the mistake.

I sing beautifully. People's faces light up when they hear me sing.

I sing more beautifully than you. People close their eyes and sway when they hear me sing.

I sing most beautifully of all. People weep when they hear my voice.

A HELPFUL HOMOPHONE BOOK

Class Activity

Guide students in following the directions below to make their own Homophone Help mini-books. Students can use them as handy resources for their own writing. Decide ahead of time if you want students to choose the homophone sets for step 7 or if you want them to use ones you've chosen based on common errors in student writing. (Suggestions: there/their/they're, it's/its, your/you're, to/too/two, threw/through, whole/hole, whose/who's) Each student will need a blank sheet of 11" x 17" paper, scissors, and one rubber band.

1. Fold a blank sheet of paper in half widthwise twice and unfold it.

2. Fold it in half lengthwise and unfold it.

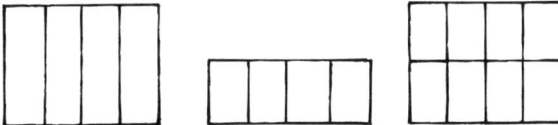

3. Fold it in half widthwise once again. Cut halfway across the middle fold line. Unfold the paper to see the center slit.

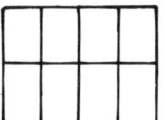 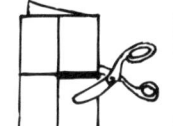 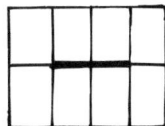

4. Fold the paper in half lengthwise once again.

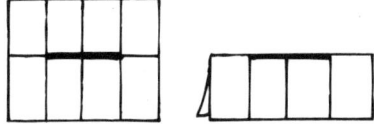

5. Hold the ends and push them toward the center to make a plus sign shape.

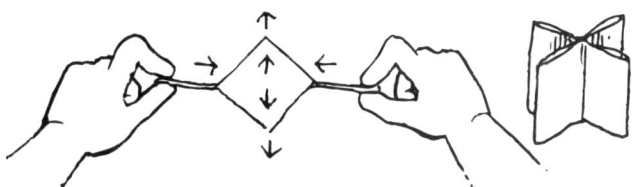

6. Stretch a rubber band around the center to make a book spine. Push the pages together to make an 8-page book. Label your cover "Homophone Help."

7. Write a set of homophones on the other seven pages. Use each word in its own sentence to show its correct usage. If there is room, illustrate one of the sentences on each page.

DOES "ALOT" BOTHER YOU A LOT?

Class Activity

If your students write "alot" rather than the correct version, "a lot," teach them this rhyme:

> *You may think it matters not;*
> *but since you don't write "alittle," don't write "alot."*

It Does Matter!

Many people use the **contraction** *don't* when they should use *doesn't*.

Wrong: *That bird don't know how to fly. Yes, it do!*
Correct: *That bird doesn't know how to fly. Yes, it does!*

Read each pair of sentences. Rewrite the pair correctly. Read aloud your correct sentences twice to practice speaking and hearing correct English.

1. **Wrong:** She don't get it. Yes, she do!

   Correct: _____

2. **Wrong:** He don't like it. Yes, he do!

   Correct: _____

3. **Wrong:** It don't matter. Yes, it do!

   Correct: _____

4. **Wrong:** My mom don't want me to learn this. Yes, she do!

   Correct: _____
   _____

5. **Wrong:** My dad don't notice if I speak incorrectly. Yes, he do!

   Correct: _____
   _____

6. **Wrong:** My family don't care about school. Yes, it do!

   Correct: _____
   _____

Use *don't* if the subject is a plural subject (the boys, we, they, Leah and Molly) or is the pronoun *I* or *you*. Write three sentences of your own that correctly use *don't*.

_____
_____

Track and Field Day

Some verbs are **irregular**. They form their past tenses and past participles in irregular ways.

Present — *Today is Track and Field Day for the fourth graders.*
Past — *Yesterday was Track and Field Day for the fifth graders.*
Past participle — *The first week of May has been Track and Field Week at our school for years.*

Read these sentences. Write the correct past tense verb or past participle. Clue: A past participle is used with the helping verbs *have, has,* or *had.*

1. Fifth-grade Track and Field Day _____ with the high jump. (began, begun)
2. Many parents had _____ to cheer us on. (came, come)
3. I had just _____ my first jump (began, begun)
   when I _____ my mom and dad. (saw, seen)
4. I _____ nervous and ran right into the bar. (got, gotten)
5. It _____ embarrassing! (was, been)
6. Next, we _____ to the long-jump area. (went, gone)
7. Since I had already _____ my parents, I did not mess up. (saw, seen)
8. I _____ my school's long-jump record for fifth graders. (broke, broken)
9. After the jumping events, we _____ the 50-meter dash. (did, done)
10. I am not a fast runner, but my friend _____ in second place. (came, come)
11. At the softball throw, I only _____ the ball 41 feet. (threw, thrown)
12. I had _____ it farther than that in third grade! (threw, thrown)
13. For the last event, we _____ a mile. (ran, run)
14. I _____ I wouldn't earn a ribbon, (knew, known)
    but I _____ run the whole way. (did, done)
15. Finally, Track and Field Day _____ over. (was, been)
16. It had _____ a fun and exhausting day. (was, been)

Name _____

Singular or Plural?

In order to use the correct present tense form of a verb, you need to know if the subject is singular or plural. Use this page as a reference sheet.

A **collective noun** names a group of people, animals, or things. It is usually a singular noun.

audience	colony	mob
band	committee	pack
batch	country	pile
bouquet	crew	pod
brood	family	pride
bunch	fleet	school
bundle	flock	set
cache	gaggle	stack
cast	group	string
chorus	herd	swarm
class	host	team
clump	jury	tribe
cluster	litter	troop

Examples:
Our class goes on lots of field trips.
A pod of whales is swimming this way.
That bunch of seaweed looks strange.

An **indefinite pronoun** takes the place of a noun in a general way.

- These indefinite pronouns are singular:

anybody	everyone	nothing
anyone	everything	one
anything	neither	somebody
each	nobody	someone
either	no one	something
everybody		

Examples:
Everyone likes practicing for the play.
Few are going to have singing parts.
All of the scenery group is here today.
All of them are working hard.

- These indefinite pronouns are plural:

both	many	several
few	others	

- These indefinite pronouns can be singular or plural depending on the noun they represent:

all	more	none
any	most	some

That Sounds Terrible!

Read Paul's story. Fill in the missing pronouns.

Subject Pronoun	Object Pronoun
I	me
you	you
he	him
she	her
it	it
we	us
they	them

At my school fifth graders may take band and learn to play an instrument. I didn't know which instrument to choose, so _____ asked my parents.

"Hey, Mom, what instrument did _____ play when you were a kid?"

_____ replied, "I played the clarinet and the alto saxophone."

"How about _____, Dad?" I asked.

"I was an expert at the trombone until my parents made _____ quit."

"Why did _____ make you quit?"

"Their exact words were '_____ can't take this noise anymore. You are driving _____ buggy. When are _____ going to start practicing and learn to play music?' "

"Don't believe _____, Paul," said my mom. "He's joking."

"_____'s the truth!" cried my dad. "Call up Gran and Papa. Ask _____."

So I called my grandparents. Dad was right. They did make _____ quit because _____ never practiced.

That helped _____ make up my mind. I decided to play the trombone. My mom asked me why. I told _____, "No matter how bad _____ sound, I'll still sound better than Dad did!"

Name_____

Who or Whom?

Use **who** when the pronoun refers to the subject.
Clue: Think to yourself, Would *he, she,* or *they* work as a similar pronoun?

Who is playing the lead role in Annie*? Alana is playing the lead. She is playing the lead.*

Use **whom** when the pronoun receives the action of the verb or is the object of a preposition.
Clue: Think to yourself, Would *him, her,* or *them* work as a similar pronoun?

Whom did Ms. Shaw choose for assistant directors?
Ms. Shaw chose Barrett and Tanya. Ms. Shaw chose them.
The greeting in Zoe's business letter was "To whom it may concern."
The letter concerned Mr. Ravik, the owner of the company. The letter concerned him.

For each sentence below, fill in the correct pronoun.

1. _____ is your favorite singer? (Who, Whom)

   _____ is my favorite singer. (She, Her)

2. To _____ should I send this letter? (who, whom)

   I should send this letter to _____. (he, him)

3. _____ would you like to invite to your party? (Who, Whom)

   I would like to invite _____. (they, them)

4. _____ knows where the Nile River is located? (Who, Whom)

   _____ knows where the Nile River is located. (He, Him)

5. With _____ do you want to be partners? (who, whom)

   I want to be partners with _____. (she, her)

6. _____ has finished their rough draft already? (Who, Whom)

   _____ have finished their rough draft already. (They, Them)

7. _____ drew this picture of the shuttle? (Who, Whom)

   _____ drew this picture of the shuttle. (She, Her)

8. _____ did we elect vice-president of our class? (Who, Whom)

   We elected _____ vice-president. (he, him)

Name_____

Doesn't Nobody Know...?

A **double negative** is a sentence with two negative words. To fix a double negative, take out one of the negative words or change one to its positive form.

Double negative: *My mom won't let neither of my two friends come over.*

Correct version: *My mom will let neither of my two friends come over.*

Correct version: *My mom won't let either of my two friends come over.*

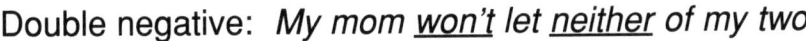

Read each sentence.
Cross out one of the negative words.
Write its positive replacement when needed.

Doesn't ~~nobody~~ know how to speak correctly? __anybody__

1. When it comes to grammar, my sister doesn't know nothing. _____
2. You shouldn't never make fun of your teachers. _____
3. None of the dinosaurs are alive no more. _____
4. I can't find my homework nowhere. _____
5. You don't do nothing right! _____
6. My brother does not want nobody to come in his room. _____
7. Goldilocks doesn't have no manners. _____
8. I don't like no one on my soccer team. _____
9. Doesn't no one have anything to do? _____
10. You may not have none of my cookies. _____
11. My dog couldn't never understand what I was saying. _____
12. When I grow up, I am not never going to make my kids eat spinach. _____
13. I have not seen nobody in the principal's office today. _____
14. Our class didn't like neither of those choices. _____
15. There is not nobody smarter than I am. _____

FS123304 Grammar Made Simple Grade 5 ▪ © Frank Schaffer Publications, Inc.   reproducible   **53**

Name _____

Orky, Dorky, and Zorky

An adjective describes a noun.
An adverb modifies a verb.
Both adjectives and adverbs
can be compared.

Read each sentence.
Fill in the circle next to the
correct adjective or adverb.
Use the charts as a guide.

Adjective	Comparing two	Comparing more than two
good	better	best
bad	worse	worst

Adverb	Comparing two	Comparing more than two
well	better	best
badly	worse	worst

1. Orky, Dorky, and Zorky are ___ friends.
   ○ good
   ○ well

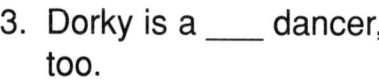

2. Orky dances ___.
   ○ good
   ○ well

3. Dorky is a ___ dancer, too.
   ○ good
   ○ better

4. Zorky is the ___ dancer of all.
   ○ better
   ○ best

5. Zorky can dance well, but she skates ___.
   ○ bad
   ○ badly

6. Orky skates even ___ than Zorky.
   ○ worse
   ○ worser

7. Dorky is the ___ skater of the three.
   ○ worse
   ○ best

8. Dorky is a ___ driver.
   ○ bad
   ○ badly

9. Zorky drives ___.
   ○ good
   ○ well

10. Orky is the ___ driver on Planet Ork!
    ○ worse
    ○ worst

11. Like most Orklings, Zorky is a ___ storyteller.
    ○ good
    ○ well

12. Orky is a ___ storyteller than Zorky.
    ○ gooder
    ○ better

13. Dorky tells stories ___ of all.
    ○ best
    ○ bestest

Watch Their Ball!

Read each sentence.
Write the correct missing word.
When you choose a contraction,
check if it is correct by reading
aloud the two words it stands for.

Contraction	Possessive
it's (it is)	its (belongs to it)
you're (you are)	your (belongs to you)
they're (they are)	their (belongs to them)

Class, __it's__ Force and Motion Experiment Day. (its, it's)

1. The first group to do _____ demonstration will be Natalie's group. (its, it's)
2. Natalie, _____ group is doing the floating ball experiment. (your, you're)
3. _____ going to need a hair dryer and a ping pong ball. (Your, You're)
4. _____ over in that supply box. (Their, They're)
5. Class, watch what _____ amazing hair dryer can do. (their, they're)
6. What evidence can you see of _____ force? (its, it's)
7. Class, can you think of three forces acting on _____ ping pong ball? (their, they're)
8. One is the force of gravity—_____ pulling the ball toward the ground. (its, it's)
9. _____ right, Meng. (Your, You're)
10. Another force is air pressure—_____ pushing down on the ball. (its, it's)
11. Lauren, _____ answer is correct also. (your, you're)
12. Natalie, can _____ group tell us the third force? (your, you're)
13. We think _____ the upward force coming from the hair dryer. (its, it's)
14. Good. Class, now _____ going to slowly move the hair dryer next to the wall. (their, they're)
15. What do you think will happen to _____ ping pong ball? (their, they're)

The Tortoise and the Hair *(Hare)*

Read this story Brandy wrote. Can you find the 25 homophones she deliberately misused? Underline them. Write the correct word in the side margin. The first one is done for you.

there

Once upon a time their was a very boastful hare. He was always making fun of Tortoise.

"Tortoise, eye think a growing flour moves faster than you do," Hare would tease.

Finally, Tortoise got tired of Hare's insults. "I may bee slow, but I could beet you in a race."

"Ha, ha, ha, Tortoise! There is know weigh you could beat the fastest feat in all the land," said Hare, and he lifted won big foot for emphasis. "Isle race you to prove it."

"Fine," said Tortoise, "tomorrow wee shall race."

The next day animals from near and far came to watch the grate race. Even though most thought Hare wood win, they came to cheer on there friend Tortoise.

"On you're mark, get set, go!" called Bare.

Hare bolted away, leaving Tortoise in the dust. For a half our, Hare leaped, zoomed, and zipped threw the course. Hare was sew far ahead he decided to take a nap. While Hare slept, Tortoise plodded along slowly. Over and over again he chanted, "Right foot, left foot, left foot, write foot."

A noise woke Hare. He wondered too himself, "What is that sound? I'd better run." Hare raced to the finish line only to sea a tired but happy Tortoise being congratulated bye his friends. Four once, the loud-mouthed Hare had nothing two say.

Name _____

Don't Mix Them Up!

The word pairs below look and sound similar, but have different meanings. Write the definition of each word. Use a dictionary if needed. Then fill in the circle next to the correct word for each sentence.

accept _____

except _____

angel _____

angle _____

breath _____

breathe _____

conscience _____

conscious _____

desert _____

dessert _____

finally _____

finely _____

picture _____

pitcher _____

---

1. Please fill this ____ with water.
   ○ picture
   ○ pitcher

2. The ____ measured 90°.
   ○ angel
   ○ angle

3. Coyotes live in the ____.
   ○ desert
   ○ dessert

4. I like every flavor ____ mint chip.
   ○ accept
   ○ except

5. He chopped the onions so ____ that I couldn't taste them.
   ○ finally
   ○ finely

6. The doctor told her patient to ____ deeply.
   ○ breath
   ○ breathe

7. You know the right thing to do—listen to your ____.
   ○ conscience
   ○ conscious

Mechanics

Oral language does not involve mechanics, but written language does. Mechanics include the rules for capitalization and punctuation that help a reader decipher writing. The more students read and write, the greater their needs and the greater their opportunities for learning the mechanics of English.

E-MAIL ADDRESSES
Partner Activity

E-mail and website addresses may confuse the issue of capitalization. Write a few e-mail or website addresses on the chalkboard. Elicit ideas from students on what the letters, abbreviations, and words stand for. Write those words around the address connecting them with arrows. Capitalize the proper nouns they represent. (http stands for HyperText Transfer Protocol. It is the "language" of the web. It is the server that takes requests from people using the web and fulfills them.)

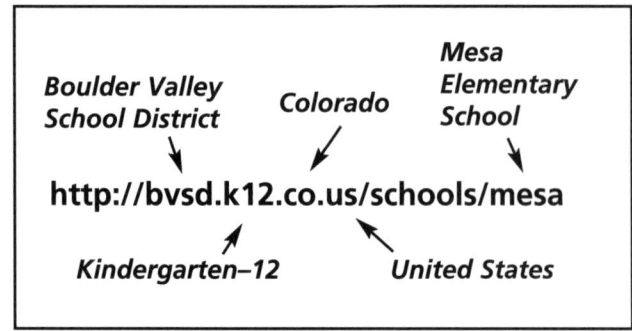

The next time your class is using the Internet, direct pairs to copy three e-mail or website addresses (including their own if available). Have them decipher the letters, abbreviations, and words, and write the corresponding proper nouns around them.

NEW YORKERS, NEW JERSEYITES
Class Activity

Connect U.S. geography with a lesson on capitalization (and suffixes!). Review with students that names of states are capitalized. Ask students what people from your state are called. On the chalkboard, write both the state name and the nickname for state citizens. Point out that they are both capitalized. Challenge the class to find the nicknames for each state's citizens. Decide if you want this to be a partner project, a group challenge, or a class activity. Direct all students to write the names of the states in alphabetical order. Then have them write the citizen nickname beside each state name. After you have compiled a master list, you may want to do a mini-lesson on suffixes. Encourage students to look for patterns, asking questions such as these: Which states added the suffix *-ers*? Which states added the suffix *-ns*?

TO CAPITALIZE OR NOT? *Class Activity*

While prose has strict rules for capitalization, poetry allows the poet to bend the rules to fit the mood. Copy onto chart paper several poems that use different styles of capitalization. For example, you might copy these three poems from *Celebrate America in Poetry and Art* edited by Nora Panzer (Hyperion Books, 1994): "Song of the Builders" by Jessie Wilmore Murton (each line begins with a capital letter), "Raising My Hand" by Antler (some lines begin with a capital letter, indented lines do not), and "Knoxville, Tennessee" by Nikki Giovanni (only *I*, the first word in the poem, is capitalized). Discuss with students why they think each poet chose to capitalize the poem as he or she did. For a follow-up homework activity, direct students to find poems they like and copy them onto paper, matching the capitalization styles and indentation styles exactly. Provide bulletin board space for students to display their poems.

THE KIDS PREFER AWARDS *Group Activity*

Teach or review guidelines for capitalizing and punctuating titles.

1. The first word and last word in a title are always capitalized.
2. Articles *(a, an, the)*, short conjunctions *(and)*, and short prepositions *(in, of, to, for . . .)* in the middle of a title are not capitalized.
3. All other words are capitalized.
4. Titles of books, magazines, newspapers, movies, plays, and TV shows are underlined or italicized.
5. Titles of articles, poems, short stories, and songs are written in quotation marks.

For the category Kids Favorite Song, we choose . . .

Then divide the class into small groups. Tell groups they are to create lists of Kids Prefer Awards for books, songs, magazines, movies, and TV shows. Each group can decide its own categories, but must give a total of 10 awards. Require each group to submit lists of awards and recipients. Let each group choose three awards to announce to the class.

DEAR . . . *Class Activity*

Letter writing can be used to teach or practice almost every rule of capitalization and punctuation. Moreover, it teaches students a valuable practice—writing to communicate. Brainstorm types of letters and reasons why someone might write a letter. Involve students in letter-writing activities to match your list throughout the year. Balance the activities so that some letters are actually mailed and others are written simply for fun. Use the reproducible on page 67 as a reference for students.

friendly letters, invitations, thank-you notes, letters to the editor, fan mail, requests, orders, apologies, condolences, birthday cards, complaints, congratulations, love letters, "Dear John" letters, postcards . . .

PUNCTUATION POSTERS

Class Activity

Ask the class to name the punctuation marks they know. List both the marks and their names on the chalkboard. Tell students they have one week to find, cut out, and sort into lunch bags or envelopes as many examples of the punctuation marks as they can. Explain that each item must use the mark in a different way—i.e. only one example of a period used at the end of a statement. Brainstorm a list of possible sources: mail, newspaper, food packaging, catalogs, and so on. When students have completed the assignment, discuss each punctuation mark in turn. For each mark, write a list telling how it is used. Let students glue their examples beside the corresponding item on the list.

.	*period*
,	*comma*
?	*question mark*
!	*exclamation mark*
'	*apostrophe*
" "	*quotation marks*
:	*colon*
;	*semicolon*
-	*hyphen*
—	*dash*
( )	*parentheses*

WE THE PEOPLE

Class Activity

The Preamble to the Constitution of the United States of America is a wonderful model sentence to present when teaching the need for using commas in a series. You may want to introduce the lesson by showing students Mike Wilkins's piece of art "Preamble." It is the Preamble formed using license plates in alphabetical order from all 50 states. For example, the word *States* is shown on a license plate as "ST8S." You can find a picture of the artwork and the complete written text of the Preamble in *Celebrate America in Poetry and Art* edited by Nora Panzer (Hyperion Books, 1994). Have students try to decipher the message in the artwork. Then provide each student with a copy of the Preamble. Talk about how the commas help the reader break up the sentence into smaller parts that are more easily understood. You may also want to share Peter Spier's picture book version of the Preamble—*We the People* (Doubleday, 1987). It uses illustrations of both historical and modern-day scenes to interpret each phrase.

Once the general meaning of the Preamble is understood, you can point out the grammatical structure of the sentence. Help students see how the commas separate parallel items in a series: " . . . <u>form</u> a more perfect union, <u>establish</u> justice, <u>insure</u> domestic tranquility, . . ." If you like, have students create their own banner of the Preamble. (You may want to work on the cafeteria or gym floor for space.) Give each child a long strip of paper (cut from butcher paper or an industrial paper towel roll). Direct students to neatly write the entire Preamble, including punctuation, at the tops of their papers. Have them trim off any extra paper at the right edge. Then have students illustrate the ideas below each matching phrase.

POETIC PUNCTUATION *Partner Activity*

Choose some humorous poems you enjoy and read them aloud to students. Some possible poems, from Shel Silverstein's *Where the Sidewalk Ends* (Harper & Row, 1974), are "Hat," "The Crocodile's Toothache," "Jimmy Jet and His TV Set." Ask students what makes each poem appealing and write their responses. (humor, word choice, rhyme, rhythm . . .) Point out that those are important components when *listening* to a poem. Ask students what else is important if you are *reading* a poem. Guide them as needed in recognizing that the mechanics involved—capitalization, indentation, and punctuation—all combine to help the reader interpret a poem. Copy one or more of the poems you read aloud onto the chalkboard or an overhead transparency. Discuss how the mechanical elements helped you read the poem.

Then gather a collection of poetry books. Let students work with partners, choose books, and take turns reading aloud poems to each other. Encourage students to look for clues in the mechanics of the poem that will help them read it expressively. Invite pairs to come to the front of the class to read aloud their favorite poem.

NEW! NOISY! NUTRITIONAL! *Partner Activity*

Ask students to bring empty snack boxes—crackers, granola bars, and so on—to class. Have students work with partners, reading and comparing the packaging. Hold a class discussion about what companies do to make their product appealing. Have students give examples from their boxes. Challenge pairs to think of new food products. Have them cover one of their boxes with paper and design the packaging for their product. Require students to write, edit, and proofread their advertising copy on scratch paper before writing on the box. Display the finished packages on a counter, with a sign labeled "Would You Buy These?"

THE DRAMATIC DASH *Class Activity*

A dash is a fun punctuation mark to use. In some ways it serves the same purpose as other punctuation marks, but with a bit more flair. For example, a comma signals the reader to pause. A dash can also show a pause or interruption. A colon is sometimes used to introduce a list; a dash can be used in that role, too. In addition, a dash is often used at the end of an interruption that is not continued.

I found my favorite pajamas—the ones with bunny feet—and packed them in my bag.
Bring these things to the slumber party—sleeping bag, pajamas, flashlight, and dress-up clothes.
We were sneaking into the living room when—

Have students look in chapter books or poetry books for paragraphs or poems that use dashes. Have students copy the passages and identify the sources. Let students meet in small groups to compare their results. Encourage students to think about using the dash—sparingly—in their own writing.

SHE'LL BE COMIN' ROUND THE MOUNTAIN

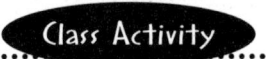

Review with students the different purposes they already know for the apostrophe (contractions, possessive nouns). Teach them that an apostrophe can also signal missing letters or numbers within a single word or numeral. Write these examples on the chalkboard for students to decipher:

We went fishin' last weekend. (fishing)
They were playing 'possum. (opossum)
Rock 'n' roll (and)
The Spirit of '76 (1776)
The Crash of '29 (1929)

Extend the lesson with a music activity. Sing the song "She'll Be Comin' Round the Mountain." Either find and analyze the lyrics in a music book or challenge students to write the lyrics from memory (correctly using apostrophes, of course!).

"LEAVE THE PUDDING ALONE," . . .

Punctuating dialogue is one of the trickiest skills to master. Before students apply the rules they learn to their own writing, have them analyze existing literature. Begin by reading aloud an interesting passage with dialogue. Suggestion: Jim Trelease's *Hey! Listen to This: Stories to Read Aloud* (Penguin, 1992) contains passages from nearly 50 stories, including the entertaining excerpt "The Pudding Like a Night on the Sea" from Ann Cameron's *The Stories Julian Tells*. Next, copy part of the passage onto the chalkboard, including its punctuation. Have students point out the different marks and guide them as needed in identifying why each is used. Point out how a line is indented each time the speaker changes. Then direct students to work in small groups. Have them find conversations in picture books or chapter books to read aloud within their groups, letting each group member take a different part. Then have them analyze the punctuation. Write questions like these to help guide the discussions: *Where do quotation marks go? Where does a period go? Where does a question mark or an exclamation mark go? Where do commas go? When do commas replace a period?* Meet with each group to assess and foster their understanding of the marks.

For a follow-up computer activity, let students use their passages to create worksheets for their classmates. Have students type 10-line passages, citing the story sources and their authors. Direct students to carefully proofread the passages for correct spelling, capitalization, punctuation, and indenting. Next have them copy and paste their passages onto new pages in their files. Direct students to leave one copy as is for an answer key and to remove the punctuation marks from the other copy. They can then print the incomplete passages for their classmates to punctuate.

My Favorite...

Write your favorite(s) for each category.
Follow these tips for capitalization and punctuation:
- Capitalize the names of people, animals, places, and things—Miss Walker, Fido, Texas, Scrabble®.
- Do not capitalize common nouns—yellow, math, pizza, volleyball, kangaroo.
- Capitalize the first, last, and major words in titles—"America the Beautiful."
- Underline the titles of books, magazines, plays, movies, and TV shows—<u>Titanic</u>.
- Put quotation marks around the titles of songs and poems—"This Land Is Your Land."

People _____

Animals _____

Color _____

Food _____

School subject _____

Sport or game _____

Place _____

City _____

State _____

Artist _____

Author _____

Book _____

Poem _____

Song _____

Singer or group _____

Movie _____

TV program _____

Thing to do that is free _____

Name _____

Guess My Abbreviation

An **abbreviation** is a short way of writing a word or group of words.
An abbreviation usually has a period (**.**) at the end of it.
If the word begins with a capital letter, its abbreviation should also.

Play this game with a partner.

1. Player A chooses an abbreviation from the list below.
2. Player B asks exactly five questions about the abbreviation that can be answered *yes* or *no*.
   Example: Does your abbreviation begin with a capital letter?
3. Player B gets three tries to guess the abbreviation and earn points.
   First guess is right: 3 points   Second guess is right: 2 points
   Third guess is right: 1 point   All guesses are wrong: 0 points
4. Switch roles and play an even number of rounds. The player with the most points wins.

Does it begin with an "a"?

a.m. or A.M.	*ante meridiem* (before noon)	kg	kilogram	oz.	ounce, ounces
Apr.	April	km	kilometer	p.; pp.	page; pages
Aug.	August	L	liter	p.m. or P.M.	*post meridiem* (after noon)
Ave.	Avenue	lb.	pound; pounds		
Blvd.	Boulevard	misc.	miscellaneous	Pres.	President
cm	centimeter	ml	milliliter	qt.	quart; quarts
Co.	Company	Mon.	Monday	Rd.	Road
Dec.	December	Mr.	Mister	Rep.	Representative
Dr.	Doctor; Drive	Mrs.	Mistress	Rev.	Reverend
E.	East	Mt.	Mountain; Mount	S. or So.	South
etc.	*et cetera* (and so forth)	N.	North	Sat.	Saturday
		No.	number; North	Sen.	Senator
Feb.	February	Nov.	November	Sept.	September
Fr.	Father	Oct.	October	Sr.	Senior; Sister
Fri.	Friday			St.	Street; Saint
ft.	foot; feet			Sun.	Sunday
Gen.	General			Thurs.	Thursday
Gov.	Governor			Tues.	Tuesday
in.	inch; inches			vs. or v.	versus
Jan.	January			W.	West
Jr.	Junior			Wed.	Wednesday
				yd.	yard; yards

The First Six Presidents

Use a **comma** (,) to separate the month and day from the year.
George Washington was born on February 22, 1732.
Use a **comma** (,) to separate a city or county from a state.
He was born in Westmoreland County, Virginia.

Fill in the missing commas in this chart.

President	Born	Birthplace	Died
George Washington	Feb. 22 1732	Westmoreland County Virginia	Dec. 14 1799
John Adams	Oct. 30 1735	Braintree Massachusetts	Jul. 4 1826
Thomas Jefferson	Apr. 13 1743	Albemarle County Virginia	Jul. 4 1826
James Madison	Mar. 16 1751	Port Conway Virginia	Jun. 28 1836
James Monroe	Apr. 28 1758	Westmoreland County Virginia	Jul. 4 1831
John Quincy Adams	Jul. 11 1767	Braintree Massachusetts	Feb. 23 1848

Write five questions that could be answered using information from the chart. Each question should include a comma within a date or within the birthplace.
Write the full names of months—not abbreviations.
Example: *Which two presidents died on July 4, 1826?*

1. _____

2. _____

3. _____

4. _____

5. _____

Name _____

Write a Check

Write the name of the company or person who will get your money.

Use a comma to separate the day from the year.

Write the dollar amount as words, capitalizing the first word. Use a hyphen to separate tens and ones. Write the word *and* followed by the cents written as a fraction.

Write the amount as a number. Use a decimal point (period) to separate dollars from cents.

Date __Aug. 10, 2001__

Pay to the order of __Wave World__ | $ __54.25__

__Fifty-four and 25/100__ _____ Dollars

Grammar Bank

Memo __Malcolm's Birthday__   __Alexander D. Miser__

Optional: Write a note telling the purpose of the check.

Sign your name here.

Think of two places where you would want to write a check to buy something or pay for admission. Fill in these checks, using the check above as a guide. Choose an amount that is between $21.00 and $99.00 and that is <u>not</u> a multiple of 10—$30, $40, $50, and so on.

Date _____

Pay to the order of _____ | $ _____

_____ Dollars

Grammar Bank

Memo _____   _____

Date _____

Pay to the order of _____ | $ _____

_____ Dollars

Grammar Bank

Memo _____   _____

66 reproducible   FS123304 Grammar Made Simple Grade 5 • © Frank Schaffer Publications, Inc.

Name _____

Writing Letters

Use this page as a reference for writing letters.

Friendly Letter

Date	June 1, 2004
Salutation	Dear Louie,
Body	Guess what? I finally have enough money to buy a Zapper! Tomorrow my mom is taking me to the store. When you come out, we can play with it. See you soon!
Closing Signature	Your best friend, Tony

Business Letter

Envelope

Anthony Accomazzo
123 W. Elm St.
Anytown, CA 90505

    Ms. Olivia Gadget
    President
    Superduper Toys
    P.O. Box 1466
    Phoenix, AZ 85012

Heading
(Sender's address and date)

123 W. Elm St.
Anytown, CA 90505
June 3, 2004

Inside Address
(Recipient's name, title, company, and address)

Ms. Olivia Gadget
President
Superduper Toys
P.O. Box 1466
Phoenix, AZ 85012

Salutation

Dear Ms. Gadget:

Body

Yesterday I bought a Superduper Zapper. I had saved my allowance for six weeks to buy it. It broke the first time I used it!

Please send me a new Zapper or a refund. I have included a copy of my receipt. Thank you.

Closing

Sincerely yours,

Signature
(Sender's full name)

Anthony Accomazzo

Dear Mom and Dad

Kelly's teacher had students write a letter to someone about their field trip. Read this letter. There are 25 words that need to be capitalized but are not. Underline three times the first letter in those words.

Example: d̲ear

---

april 14, 2000

dear Mom and dad,

   Today my class went on a field trip to the denver Museum of natural History. we saw an exhibit called "remember the Children: Daniel's Story." It was about a Jewish boy who grew up in germany in the 1930s and survived the Holocaust. Daniel was not a real boy, but his story was based on real events.

   The exhibit had four parts. The first was called "daniel's House." it was a display of a typical German home.

   The next part was titled "scary Changes." It showed how the nazi Party made unfair rules for Jewish people. in that part, Daniel wrote in his diary that even his teacher at school makes fun of him.

   the third part was "The ghetto." Daniel's family and other jewish families were forced to move into a small section of another city. They were fenced in and couldn't leave.

   The last part was titled "the concentration Camp." Daniel's family was sent to a concentration camp. many Jewish people were killed there, but not daniel.

   at the end of the exhibit, the museum had volunteers who talked with us about what we saw. Even though it was not a fun trip, i am glad we went. We learned a lot about the holocaust.

                                             love,
                                             kelly

Ski Club

Read this letter and envelope. Fill in the missing punctuation marks:

- ☐ 4 commas
- ☐ 8 periods
- ☐ 2 question marks
- ☐ 2 exclamation marks

February 4 2002

Dear Maddy

    Yesterday I got to go skiing for the first time. It was great Have you ever skied

    My school has a ski club We go skiing four Saturdays in February. The ski area is about two hours away from here. We had to meet in the school parking lot at 6:15 a.m to catch the bus! It was hard getting up that early

    I was in a group with six other kids who were 10 or 11 and had never skied before We had two instructors. They were funny. In the morning we stayed on the easiest slope It's called the Bunny Hill. We learned to "make a pizza"—that's when you point your skis together to make an upside down V-shape. The wider your V, the slower you go After lunch we got to ride the chair lift. That was so fun

    Maybe if you come visit us, we could go skiing together. Would you like to do that   Write me back

                         Your cousin
                         Nora

Nora DeWitt
35 Powderhorn Ln.
Louisville CO 80027

        Maddy DeWitt
        967 Cumberland Ave
        Columbus, GA 31907

Cat Got Your Tongue?

A **comma** (,) tells the reader to pause.

Use a comma to separate the person being spoken to from what is being said.
   Examples: *Class, today we are going to act out idioms.*
       Will you explain what an idiom is, Mrs. McCreary?

Use a comma after *Yes, No,* or other introductory words and after an interjection at the beginning of a sentence.
   Examples: *Yes, Brian, I will. An idiom is a phrase or expression that means something different from its exact words.*
       Oops, I forgot the handout.

Read each set of sentences. Add the missing commas.

1. Julia watch me throw this clock out the window.
       Why are you doing that Mackenzie?
   I want to see if time flies!

2. Hunter do you have a mirror?
       No Thomas why do you want one?
   I want to see if the cat's got my tongue!

3. Janey and Michelle are you sick?
       No we just painted our faces green.
   Egad what did you do that for?
       You said we were two peas in a pod.

4. Snort-snort!
       Matthew are you snorting like a pig?
   Yes Nicole.
       Why are you doing that Matthew?
   My dad told me to go whole hog on my project.

5. Will you pretend you are lightning Fernando?
       OK if you want me to. Why am I doing this Alma?
   I need to steal someone's thunder!

6. Gross that is disgusting!
       Yes it is. Don't ever make me pay through the nose again Mrs. McCreary!

Camp Porcupine

Use a **comma** (,) to separate words in a series of three or more items.
Gwen, Vanessa, Corey, and Sean want to go to camp.
Camp Porcupine has woodlands, fields, and a lake to explore.

Use a **colon** (:) to introduce a list.
Mail these items to the office three weeks before camp: sign-up form, health form, activity form, emergency card, and final payment.

Read these sentences. Add the missing commas and colons.

1. Pack these things in a backpack for the bus trip a snack a water bottle sunscreen and a hat.
2. Do not bring these items to Camp Porcupine gum candy money and electronic gadgets.
3. Campers counselors and activity leaders are assigned to units at Camp Porcupine.
4. Each unit has these structures six camper tents two staff tents two bathrooms and one shower house.
5. Eagle Coyote and Grizzly Bear are the three girls' units.
6. The boys' units are Fox Hawk and Elk.
7. You must do these lodge chores when your unit has meal duty set the tables serve food clear the dishes clean the tables and sweep the floors.
8. Gwen arrived at camp met her counselor found her gear and hiked to her unit.
9. Sean's tent mates were Antwan Steve and Josh.
10. The campers got to choose three of these water activities to do swimming canoeing kayaking water skiing or fishing.
11. Corey's unit spent the first day doing the obstacle course archery and outdoor cooking.
12. Vanessa liked riding grooming and feeding the horses.
13. The three-legged race the shaving-cream fight and the goofy-face contest were all part of the Wacky Wednesday activities.
14. The evening camp activities usually included most of these five things singing storytelling skits a night hike and a campfire snack.

Name _____

Watch Out, Goldilocks!

Use **quotation marks** (" ") to show the exact words a speaker says.
  Papa Bear exclaimed, "Someone's been eating my porridge!"

Use a **comma** (,) to set off the exact words a speaker says from the rest of the sentence.
  "Someone's been eating my porridge, too," chimed in Mama Bear.
  "Someone's been eating my porridge," sobbed Baby Bear, "and now it's all gone."

If a speaker's exact words need a **question mark** or **exclamation mark**, write the mark inside the quotation marks.
  Mama Bear asked, "Do you think the intruder is still here?"
  "Watch out, you nasty intruder!" shouted Baby Bear. "We're coming to get you."

Read this conversation. Write the missing punctuation marks.
Finish the conversation by writing a line each for Baby Bear and Goldilocks.

  Let's check the living room   suggested Baby Bear

  Hmmph! Someone's been sitting in my chair   growled Papa Bear

  Oh, my   gasped Mama Bear.   Someone's been sitting in my chair, too

  Quit feeling sorry for yourselves and pay attention to me   said Baby Bear as he pointed to his chair.   Whoever it was broke my chair

  Shall we check the bedroom   asked Papa Bear

  Let's go quietly   whispered Mama Bear

  Watch out, you nasty intruder   shouted Baby Bear   We're coming to get you

  Shh, BB   Mama Bear reprimanded.

  Oh, Mom   grumbled Baby Bear

  Papa Bear announced   Someone's been sleeping in my bed

  Here we go again   sighed Mama Bear   Someone's been sleeping in my bed

_____
_____
_____

What's That Noise?

Use an apostrophe (') in a contraction to show one or more letters are missing.
  don't do not   let's let us   that'd that would or that had

Use an apostrophe (') with a noun to show possession.
  Jeremy's report   the girls' backpacks   the children's projects

Each sentence contains a contraction and a possessive noun. Add the two missing apostrophes. On the line, write the two words that make up the contraction.

<u>What is</u>   What's that noise coming from the teachers' lounge?

_____ 1. Its the teachers practicing for the schools talent show!

_____ 2. Heres Rick and Matts script.

_____ 3. Lets see if we can use that kids umbrella for our skit.

_____ 4. Whatre you doing for next weeks show?

_____ 5. Were going to lip-sync the Beach Boys song "Surfing U.S.A."

_____ 6. Ask Kristens sister if shell let us borrow her CD.

_____ 7. Didnt you think the first graders skit was cute?

_____ 8. Mr. Foxs kindergarten class wouldnt stop singing at their practice.

_____ 9. Wasnt that Davids little sister who played Mother Nature?

Write two sentences of your own that contain both a contraction and a possessive noun. Punctuate them correctly.

_____
_____
_____
_____

Orphan Trains

Kenny typed his report. Now he needs your help to proofread it.
Check off (✔) each step as you do it.

☐ Underline three times the 9 letters that should be capitalized. (n̲)
☐ Write the 5 missing periods. (.)
☐ Write the 2 missing question marks. (?)
☐ Write the 3 missing commas. (,)
☐ Write the 1 missing apostrophe. (')

    Pretend you are a child living in new york city 100 years ago. Your family can not take care of you so they leave you on the streets. You have to beg for food Then some adults say they are going to help you. They place you on a train with other orphans and send you West to find a family. How would you feel

    this actually happened to about 200,000 children in the late 1800s and early 1900s They were part of the orphan train program.

    Groups of 10 to 40 orphans were put on a train One adult, called an agent, took care of them. The agents job was to place the children with families along the route. Orphan train riders found new homes in more than 30 states, including pennsylvania, Louisiana Texas, and kansas.

    The orphan train program gave many children a better life. They were welcomed into families who loved them cared for them and sent them to school.

    But not all children were so lucky Brothers or sisters were often separated. Some families took in children and forced them to work all day. when an agent learned of problems, he or she would try to find a new home for that orphan.

    some orphan train riders are still alive today. Now they are grandparents, not children They hold reunions and share their stories. How do you think they feel about the orphan train program? How would you feel

Answer Key

Page 10
1. S
2. N
3. S
4. N
5. N
6. S
7. N
8. S
9. S
10. N
11. S
12. N

Sentences will vary.

Page 11
Sentences will vary.

Page 12
1. D .
2. D or E . or !
3. Int ?
4. Imp .
5. D .
6. E !
7. Imp .
8. D or E . or !
9. Int ?
10. D .
11. Imp .
12. E !
13. Int ?
14. D .
15. Imp .

Page 13
Sentences will vary.

Page 14
1. (The pangolin's sharp scales) are made from a strange, hard form of hair.
2. (A pangolin) curls up in a ball to escape from danger.
3. (An armadillo) looks like it is covered in armor.
4. (The name armadillo) means "little armored one" in Spanish.
5. (Armadillos) have bony plates and very tough skin.
6. (A tortoise's hard shell) is its armor.
7. Inside its shell, (the tortoise) can hide from predators.
8. (The tortoise beetle) is an insect.
9. (It) has a hard shield that covers its head, legs, and body.

Sentences will vary for 10–12.
10. P
11. S
12. S

Page 15
1. Dick King-Smith; Dick King-Smith
2. I; I
3. one; My favorite one
4. book; That book
5. assignment; Our assignment
6. report; The report
7. characters; Many of the characters in King-Smith's books
8. mice; The mice in Three Terrible Trins
9. pig; The pig in Pigs Might Fly
10. project; My creative project
11. Marcus, Whitney; Marcus and Whitney

Page 16
1. can buy; can buy . . . money.
2. have; have three . . . sell.
3. spent; spent the . . . Friday.
4. stayed, worked; stayed up late and worked on our projects.
5. brought; brought beeswax with her.
6. cut, rolled; cut and rolled . . . candles.
7. helped; helped us . . . too.
8. poured; carefully poured . . . molds.
9. is coming; is coming soon.
10. decorated; decorated tiny . . . Spring."
11. made; made little . . . craft.
12. wrapped; wrapped . . . wreath.
13. glued; glued leaves . . . them.
14. will be; will be next Friday.
15. hope; hope lots . . . crafts.

Page 17
1. the beach; Sarah and Ian spent the day at Old Orchard Beach.
2. They looked for in the sand; They looked for shells and sand dollars in the sand.
3. the water; Sarah went body surfing in the cold water.
4. the waves; Ian waded in the shallow waves near shore.
5. threw seaweed at; Ian and Sarah threw seaweed at each other.
6. Sarah and Ian had lots of fun that day.

Page 18
Possible paragraph:
   Michael Jordan is my favorite athlete. I think he is the greatest basketball player ever and maybe the greatest athlete of any sport. Michael Jordan played for the Chicago Bulls. When he was on their team, the Bulls won the NBA championship six times. I think Michael is a strong, powerful player. But the reason he is so good is because whenever he plays, he gives his best. He doesn't get lazy and not try. He always tries hard. He's the greatest!

Page 30
Nouns will vary.

Page 31
1. month
2. school
3. women
4. Earth (any planet name)
5. wolves
6. kindness (or another antonym for cruelty)
7. temperature
8. telephone
9. maps
10. dusk
11. Los Angeles (any city name)
12. children
13. lizard (any reptile)
14. Japanese
15. teeth
16. foolishness (or another antonym for wisdom)
17. octopi
18. defeat
19. Mississippi (any river name)
20. Mexican

Page 32
Singular-plural noun pairs will vary.

Page 33

Dear Grandma and Grandpa,
   Thank you . . . <u>you</u> sent . . . <u>They</u> were . . . thinks <u>I</u> am . . . that <u>it</u> is . . . if <u>he</u> could . . . said, "I am . . . <u>We</u> all . . . <u>She</u> thinks . . .
   <u>We</u> are . . . <u>It</u> is coming soon. If <u>you</u> have time . . .
                    Love,
                    Liz Beth

Dear Liz Beth,
   We were . . . sent <u>us</u>. Grandma . . . liked <u>them</u> . . . picking on <u>him</u>!
   Grandma . . . visit <u>her</u> for . . .
   I talked . . . told <u>me</u> that . . . will you get <u>it</u>?
   I hope . . . We miss <u>you</u>.
                    Love,
                    Grandpa

Page 34
Sentences will vary.

Page 35
Game verbs and sentences will vary.

Page 36
   Once upon a time, there <u>was</u> a . . . her mother <u>was</u> gentle . . . when Mary <u>was</u> only five. Mary and her father <u>were</u> quite sad. "What <u>are</u> we going to do . . .
   "I <u>am</u> not worried, Father . . . We will <u>be</u> okay."
   Mary's father <u>was</u> lonely . . . Mary's stepmother, Lady Grace, <u>was</u> gentle and kind like Mary's own mother had <u>been</u>. But alas, Lady Grace <u>was</u> ill . . .
   "What <u>am</u> I going to do?" sobbed her father.
   "<u>Be</u> brave, Father!" admonished Mary.
   Once again . . . Lady Evila, <u>was</u> actually nice. Mary had <u>been</u> expecting . . . and <u>was</u> pleasantly surprised. But guess what? Yes, you <u>are/were</u> right. Lady Evila <u>was</u> a sickly creature and died, too.
   "What <u>is</u> going . . . here?" . . .
   "I think we are <u>being</u> tormented . . . Father!" realized Mary.
   Mary <u>was</u> quite right . . . Lady Bullybrains, <u>was</u> rough, mean, and healthy.

What <u>are</u> Mary and her father going to do? Will they ever <u>be</u> happy?

Page 37

began	gave
bitten	gone
break	grow
brought	hid
bought	known
choose	see
came	sang
done	spoken
draw	stand
drank	swam
driven	taken
eat	think
fell	threw
flown	worn
get	write

Page 38
Adjectives in Venn diagrams will vary.

Page 39

intelligent	intelligently
kind	kindly
fearless	fearlessly
happy	happily
successful	successfully
independent	independently
arrogant	arrogantly
careless	carelessly
possible	possibly
enthusiastic	enthusiastically
affectionate	affectionately
easy	easily
courteous	courteously
responsible	responsibly
stupid	stupidly
wise	wisely
angry	angrily
silent	silently

Page 40
1. How? <u>quickly</u>
2. When? <u>never</u>
3. Where? <u>outdoors</u>
4. When? <u>early</u>
5. How? <u>endlessly</u>
6. How? <u>carefully</u>
7. When? <u>rarely</u>
8. Where? <u>everywhere</u>
9. How? <u>unmercifully</u>
10. Where? <u>outside</u>
11. How? <u>bravely</u>
12. How? <u>cautiously</u>
13. How? <u>peacefully</u>
14. When? <u>Later</u>
15. How? <u>energetically</u>
16. How? <u>loudly</u>
17. When? <u>Then</u>

Page 41
Conjunctions may vary.
I think . . . cool. — but — I might . . . relax.
I earned . . . chores. — or — It would . . . green.
I might . . . summer. — and — I can't . . . well.
I've been . . . harder. — for, yet — Now I . . . skateboard.
I keep . . . flute. — for, yet, but — I may . . . fort.
I picked . . . grandpa's. — or — I'll be . . . grades.
I may . . . treehouse. — and — I'll use . . . muffins.

Page 48
1. She doesn't . . . she does!
2. He doesn't . . . he does!
3. It doesn't . . . it does!
4. My mom doesn't . . . she does!
5. My dad doesn't . . . he does!
6. My family doesn't . . . it does!
Sentences will vary.

Page 49
1. began
2. come
3. begun   saw
4. got
5. was
6. went
7. seen
8. broke
9. did
10. came
11. threw
12. thrown
13. ran
14. knew   did
15. was
16. been

Page 51
   At my school . . . to choose so <u>I</u> asked my parents.
   "Hey, Mom . . . did <u>you</u> play . . ." <u>She</u> replied . . .
   "How about <u>you</u>, Dad?" I asked.
   "I was . . . made <u>me</u> quit."
   "Why did <u>they</u> make you quit?"
   "Their exact words were 'We can't . . . You are driving <u>us</u> buggy. When are <u>you</u> going to . . . ' "
   "Don't believe <u>him</u> . . ."
   "<u>It</u>'s the truth! . . . Ask <u>them</u>."
   So I . . . did make <u>him</u> quit because <u>he</u> never practiced.
   That helped <u>me</u> make . . . I told <u>her</u>, "No . . . bad <u>I</u> sound . . . "

Page 52
1. Who She
2. whom him
3. Whom them
4. Who He
5. whom her
6. Who They
7. Who She
8. Whom him

Page 53
Most sentences have two ways of fixing the double negative.
1. . . . my sister knows nothing.
 . . . my sister doesn't know anything.
2. You should never make . . .
 You shouldn't ever make . . .
3. None of the dinosaurs are alive anymore.
4. I can't find my homework anywhere.
5. You do nothing right!
 You don't do anything right!
6. My brother does not want anybody to . . .
 My brother wants nobody to . . .
7. Goldilocks has no manners.
 Goldilocks doesn't have any manners.
8. I don't like anyone on . . .
 I like no one on . . .
9. Doesn't anyone have anything to do?
10. You may not have any . . .
 You may have none . . .
11. My dog could never . . .
 My dog couldn't ever . . .
12. . . . I am never going . . .
 . . . I am not ever going . . .
13. I have not seen anybody . . .
 I have seen nobody . . .
14. Our class didn't like either . . .
 Our class liked neither . . .
15. There is nobody . . .
 There is not anybody . . .

Page 54
1. good
2. well   3. good   4. best
5. badly 6. worse 7. best
8. bad   9. well   10. worst
11. good 12. better 13. best

Page 55
1. its
2. your
3. You're
4. They're
5. their
6. its
7. their
8. it's
9. You're
10. it's
11. your
12. your
13. it's
14. they're
15. their

Page 56
Once upon a time their/there was . . . Tortoise.

"Tortoise, eye/I think a growing flour/flower moves . . ." Hare would tease.

Finally . . . "I may bee/be slow, but I could beet/beat you in a race."

"Ha, ha, ha, Tortoise! There is know/no weigh/way you could beat the fastest feat/feet in all the land," said Hare and he lifted won/one big foot for emphasis. "Isle/I'll race . . ."

"Fine," said Tortoise, "tomorrow wee/we shall race."

The next day . . . the grate/great race . . . Hare wood/would win . . . to cheer on there/their friend Tortoise.

"On you're/your mark, get set, go!" called Bare/Bear.

Hare bolted . . . For a half our/hour, Hare leaped . . . zipped threw/through the course. Hare was sew/so far ahead . . . chanted, "Right foot . . . write/right foot."

A noise woke . . . wondered too/to himself . . . only to sea/see a tired . . . being congratulated bye/by his friends. Four/For once . . . nothing two/to say.

Page 57
accept—to take what is given or offered
except—leaving out; excluding
angel—spirit; very good person
angle—the space between two lines that meet or cross
breath—air that is taken into the body and let out
breathe—to take in and let out air
conscience—a feeling about what is right and wrong
conscious—awake and able to think and feel
desert—a dry land with little rain
dessert—a sweet, after-meal treat
finally—at the end; at last
finely—intricately; in tiny pieces
picture—a drawing, painting, or photograph
pitcher—a container for pouring liquids; a baseball player who throws to the batter

1. pitcher
2. angle
3. desert
4. except
5. finely
6. breathe
7. conscience

Page 63
Answers will vary.

Page 64
Abbreviation game questions will vary.

Page 65
Questions will vary.

Born	Birthplace	Died
Feb. 22, 1732	Westmoreland County, Virginia	Dec. 14, 1799
Oct. 30, 1735	Braintree, Massachusetts	Jul. 4, 1826
Apr. 13, 1743	Albemarle County, Virginia	Jul. 4, 1826
Mar. 16, 1751	Port Conway, Virginia	Jun. 28, 1836
Apr. 28, 1758	Westmoreland County, Virginia	Jul. 4, 1831
Jul. 11, 1767	Braintree, Massachusetts	Feb. 23, 1848

Page 66
Checks will vary.

ANSWER KEY

Page 68
Students should have underlined the marked letters three times:

april 14, 2000
dear Mom and dad,

Today . . . to the denver Museum of natural History. we saw an exhibit called "remember the Children: Daniel's Story." It was about a Jewish boy who grew up in germany . . .

The exhibit had four parts. The first was called "daniel's House." it was . . .

The next part was titled "scary Changes." It showed how the nazi Party made unfair rules for Jewish people. in that part . . .

the third part was "The ghetto." Daniel's family and other jewish families . . .

The last part was titled "the concentration Camp." Daniel's family was sent to a concentration camp. many Jewish people were killed there, but not daniel.

at the end of the exhibit . . . Even though it was not a fun trip, i am glad we went. We learned a lot about the holocaust.

love,
kelly

Page 69
February 4, 2002
Dear Maddy,

Yesterday . . . It was great! Have you ever skied?

My school has a ski club. We go skiing . . . It was hard getting up that early.

I was in . . . had never skied before. We had . . . In the morning we stayed on the easiest slope. It's called . . . The wider your V, the slower you go. After lunch . . . chair lift. That was so fun!

Maybe . . . Would you like to do that? Write me back.

Your cousin,
Nora

Nora DeWitt
35 Powderhorn Ln.
Louisville, CO 80027

Maddy DeWitt
967 Cumberland Ave.
Columbus, GA 31907

Page 70
1. Julia, watch . . . .
   Why . . . that, Mackenzie?
2. Hunter, do you have a mirror?
   No, Thomas, why . . . one?
3. Janey and Michelle, are . . . ?
   No, we . . . green.
   Egad, what . . . for?
4. Matthew, are . . . pig?
   Yes, Nicole.
   Why . . . that, Matthew?
5. Will . . . lightning, Fernando?
   OK, if you want me to.
   Why am I doing this, Alma?
6. Gross, that . . . ! Yes, it is.
   Don't . . . again, Mrs. McCreary!

Page 71
1. Pack . . . trip: a snack, a water bottle, sunscreen, and a hat.
2. Do . . . Porcupine: gum, candy, money, and electronic gadgets.
3. Campers, counselors, and activity leaders . . . Porcupine.
4. Each unit . . . structures: six camper tents, two staff tents, two bathrooms, and . . . house.
5. Eagle, Coyote, and Grizzly Bear are the three girls' units.
6. The boys' units are Fox, Hawk, and Elk.
7. You . . . duty: set the tables, serve food, clear the dishes, clean the tables, and . . . floors.
8. Gwen arrived at camp, met her counselor, found her gear, and hiked to her unit.
9. Sean's tentmates were Antwan, Steve, and Josh.
10. The campers . . . to do: swimming, canoeing, kayaking, water skiing, or fishing.
11. Corey's . . . obstacle course, archery, and outdoor cooking.
12. Vanessa liked riding, grooming, and feeding the horses.
13. The three-legged race, the shaving-cream fight, and the goofy-face contest . . . .
14. The . . . things: singing, storytelling, skits, a night hike, and a campfire snack.

Page 72
"Let's check the living room," suggested Baby Bear.

"Hmmph! Someone's . . . my chair," growled Papa Bear.

"Oh, my!" gasped Mama Bear. "Someone's . . . my chair, too."

"Quit feeling . . . to me," said Baby Bear . . . to his chair. "Whoever it was broke my chair!"

"Shall we check the bedroom?" asked Papa Bear.

"Let's go quietly," whispered Mama Bear.

"Watch . . . intruder!" shouted Baby Bear. "We're . . . to get you."

"Shh, BB!" Mama Bear reprimanded.

"Oh, Mom," grumbled Baby Bear.

Papa Bear announced, "Someone's . . . in my bed."

"Here we go again," sighed Mama Bear. "Someone's . . . bed."

Page 73
1. It is   It's   school's
2. Here is   Here's   Matt's
3. Let us   Let's   kid's
4. What are   What're   week's
5. We are   We're   Boys'
6. she will   Kristen's   she'll
7. Did not   Didn't   graders'
8. would not   Fox's   wouldn't
9. Was not   Wasn't   David's

Sentences will vary.

Page 74
Students should have underlined the marked letters three times:

Pretend . . . in new york city 100 years ago . . . You have to beg for food. Then some adults . . . How would you feel?

this actually happened . . . early 1900s. They . . . orphan train program.

Groups . . . were put on a train. One adult . . . The agent's job . . . including pennsylvania, Louisiana, Texas, and kansas.

The orphan train program . . . welcomed into families who loved them, cared for them, and sent them to school.

But not all children were so lucky. Brothers or sisters . . . all day. when an . . . for that orphan.

some orphan train riders are still alive today. Now they are grandparents, not children. They hold . . . How would you feel?